WAR GAMES

QUICK TAKES: MOVIES AND POPULAR CULTURE

Quick Takes: Movies and Popular Culture is a series offering succinct overviews and high-quality writing on cutting-edge themes and issues in film studies. Authors offer both fresh perspectives on new areas of inquiry and original takes on established topics.

Rebecca Bell-Metereau, *Transgender Cinema*
Blair Davis, *Comic Book Movies*
Jonna Eagle, *War Games*
Steven Gerrard, *The Modern British Horror Film*
Barry Keith Grant, *Monster Cinema*
Daniel Herbert, *Film Remakes and Franchises*
Ian Olney, *Zombie Cinema*
Valérie K. Orlando, *New African Cinema*
Stephen Prince, *Digital Cinema*
Dahlia Schweitzer, *L.A. Private Eyes*
Steven Shaviro, *Digital Music Videos*
David Sterritt, *Rock 'n' Roll Movies*
John Wills, *Disney Culture*

War Games

JONNA EAGLE

RUTGERS UNIVERSITY PRESS
New Brunswick, Camden, and Newark, New Jersey, and London

Library of Congress Cataloging-in-Publication Data

Names: Eagle, Jonna, 1968– author.
Title: War games / Jonna Eagle.
Description: New Brunswick, New Jersey :
Rutgers University Press, [2019] |
Series: Quick takes : movies and popular culture |
Includes bibliographical references and index.
Identifiers: LCCN 2019006067 | ISBN 9780813598918 (pbk. :
alk. paper) | ISBN 9780813598925 (hardcover : alk. paper)
Subjects: LCSH: War games. | War films. | Computer war games. |
War in mass media—History. | Mass media and war—History.
Classification: LCC U310 .E24 2019 | DDC 793.9/2—dc23
LC record available at https://lccn.loc.gov/2019006067

A British Cataloging-in-Publication record for this book is
available from the British Library.

∞ The paper used in this publication meets the requirements of the
American National Standard for Information Sciences—
Permanence of Paper for Printed Library Materials,
ANSI Z39.48-1992.

www.rutgersuniversitypress.org

Manufactured in the United States of America

FOR MY FAMILY, NEAR AND FAR

CONTENTS

WAR GAMES

INTRODUCTION

War. Game. The juxtaposition is striking at the outset. War is most often understood as precisely *not* a game—defined, in fact, through this distinction. "This is war!" we say, when we mean, "We're not playing around here!" And yet the very fact that we insist "War is not a game!" suggests the ease with which these categories can bleed together. Culturally and historically, the practice of war has been entangled with the practice of gaming—*practice* being the operable word, in its multiple senses of habit, training, and rehearsal. We practice at war both for the purpose of fighting it "better" and for the purpose of play. But what is the purpose of play exactly? Or the purpose of playing at war, more specifically?

As we see across this volume, war games can serve many purposes. In military contexts, they have functioned as a means of preparing for, strategizing about, and anticipating armed conflict, as well as a means of proclaiming military force and readiness. As a leisure-time activity, war games have provided an opportunity to assert mastery and control over the chaotic contingencies of violence in the past, present, and anticipated future. At the same time, these games often invite identification with this chaos as a source of both knowledge and pleasure, offering the thrilling sense of "being there" amid the violence of war.

As an expression of these contrary impulses, war games tend both to miniaturize and to immerse. We might consider this in relation to videogames, for instance, which allow us to assert control over a virtual world miniaturized on our screens but also invite us to lose ourselves in this world. Stories are central to both these functions, as they draw us in while providing structure and order to contingencies that—in actual war—exceed them. We can trace this basic tension across different modes of war gaming as they alternate between or bring together opportunities to master and to immerse ourselves in the simulated experience of war.

The present Quick Take engages these alongside other paradoxes that organize the gaming of war. The games of the title are broadly conceived as cultural and technological simulations that seek to represent—or even to reproduce—the experience of war. While some studies segregate military from recreational forms of simulation, or analog from digital ones, this account surveys a broad terrain, from live reenactments to movies, board games to videogames, in both military and recreational environments. In doing so, it is able to make connections across diverse media and contexts, to explore their interrelationships and the impulses and logics they share. The book is focused primarily on the production and circulation of war games in the context of U.S. history and culture; although other nations participate in many of the issues outlined here, their distinct contexts are beyond the scope of the present volume.

At the center of the account is a discussion of movies and television, the inclusion of which might seem surprising in a volume titled *War Games*. Though documentaries, Hollywood blockbusters, television newscasts, and reality shows do not constitute games in the traditional sense, we are incapable of accounting for the cultural force of war gaming without reckoning with these media. In addition to the way conventional war games have increasingly engaged the screen—a union manifest in the birth of videogames most conspicuously—film has offered one of the most popular, influential, and enduring forms of simulated war. From the emergence of cinema to the present, movies have issued a broad invitation into the vicarious experience of war as a source of pleasure, knowledge, and entertainment; their success has helped establish war play at the heart of our shared popular culture.

In locating movies and television alongside other forms of live and screen-based war games, this volume explores the paradox of simulation that animates these diverse forms: the striving toward a "realness" that the very premise of simulation brackets off as unattainably other. One of the central questions driving this account is how the simulation of war shapes and interacts with the real of war: both its prosecution and its immediate, embodied experience. Simulation is conventionally understood as distinct from the real that it seeks to reproduce, though these categories collapse increasingly into each other by the twenty-first century. Indeed, a reading and viewing public has long sought for the elusive real of war through its mediated representation. At the beginning of the nineteenth century, the imagination of "real war" was shaped by the ascendant mass media of the newspaper (Mieszkowski, *Watching*). In the twentieth and twenty-first centuries, it is visual media that have worked most powerfully to shape an imagination of what war is: what forms of violence define it (and which fall outside its frame); what actions it calls forth; what it feels like. Thus to trace the contours of the real, we must look paradoxically to the history of its simulation. As we shall see, the real of war has been associated most persistently with heavily stylized forms of representation and patently melodramatic structures and themes: another central paradox.

Rather than a straight chronological survey, the book is organized around three primary modes of simulating war:

live, screen based, and interactive. Although these modes overlap and intermingle in many ways, approaching the topic of war games through these conceptual categories allows for an appreciation of both the historical evolution of war simulation and some of the central issues, tensions, and themes that develop within and across its different modes. Dividing the vast field of war simulation into these three categories is not to deny their crossovers, however: tabletop games, for instance, which appear in chapter 1 on live games, are clearly an interactive form (as are combat sports, which appear there as well). And the military field exercises discussed in chapter 1 include, by the 1990s, many interactive elements. Videogames for their part, the primary focus of chapter 3, are obviously screen based and hence share central conventions and concerns with the media discussed in chapter 2.

The structure of the book allows us to trace the ascendance of new modes of simulating war while investigating the persistence of earlier forms. In chapter 1, we explore briefly the longer history of war simulation through traditional tabletop games, as well as sports and live battle reenactments, in both military and recreational contexts. As these latter examples suggest, not all gaming is oriented toward the scoring of points but as a category encompasses different kinds of play, including dressing up and firing weapons, in officially sanctioned as well as unofficial settings. These live gaming practices predate the cinema and do not rely on the mediating presence of screens, though they also persist alongside screen-based media in the twentieth and twenty-first centuries. It is to cinema (and to a lesser extent television) that we turn in chapter 2, which investigates screen-based simulations of war in the form of military documentaries, Hollywood feature films, and television broadcasts. Starting in World War II and up until the explosion of military-themed videogames in the early twenty-first century, it is cinema more than any other cultural form that shapes the popular imagination of what "real" war looks and feels like. This influence continues in the context of interactive media, the subject of chapter 3. This last chapter builds on the previous two while raising questions unique to the digital age, focusing on interactive forms including military trainers, videogames, and technologies of networked warfare. These forms extend practices and preoccupations that have come before while opening up uncharted terrain in the relationship of war simulation to war waging.

While we consider some of the central pleasures and satisfactions that war gaming has entailed, certain aspects of these pleasures remain outside our explicit focus here. One of these concerns the matter of address. While anyone can—and many do—respond to the call of war games, these games tend to construct and to hail particular kinds of subjects. Both historically and in the present, formulations of race, gender, and nation have been central to war games and to the positions with which they invite identification: positions conventionally construed as vigorous, masterful, and aggressive, though also as threatened, victimized, and vulnerable. Though these are not issues we explore directly, it is worth noting at the outset that both the fantasy of intense, embodied experience and the fantasy of a god's-eye view on the actions and fates of others are closely entwined with histories of U.S. imperialism and the subjects (and objects) they both construct and imagine.

War games have operated as part of the broader militarization of U.S. culture: the alignment of both its resources and its imagination with war. They are the progeny of military purposes, projects, and technologies. But they do not descend from these alone, tracing their origins also to more unruly practices of discovery and pleasure. The history of simulated war is thus far more complex than the overview offered here, which tracks most closely along dominant lines. In addition to the historical alignment of war gaming with what we might call an imperialist subjectivity, there are robust and varied practices that push against the strains of militarism in popular culture. These practices seek to challenge or unsettle the conventional pleasures and presumptions of war gaming, to offer up alternative kinds of enjoyment, or to open space for critical engagement or reflection. In the context of interactive media, for instance, such practices have included the intentional disruption of conventional forms of gameplay, player modifications of existing games, the appropriation of gameworlds within new mediated forms, and the design of different sorts of games entirely. While the practices of alternative and oppositional gaming are not ones we will have a chance to engage with in this survey, they are interventions well worth exploring.

1

LIVE

Across recorded history and all around the globe, human societies have played at war. These games have served as a form of recreation, a mode of memorialization, a way of adjudicating conflict, and a method of military training and planning. Games are conventionally defined as such to the extent they are constrained by a specific set of rules agreed to in advance and cordoned off in some way from the political world of which warfare itself is a part. The degree of violence they entail is likewise limited by its scope, its intensity, or both: gladiatorial contests may involve lethal violence, for instance, but spectators can be reasonably assured of their safety; and massive military field exercises may involve thousands of troops across hundreds of miles but stop short of using real bullets. In this way, games are understood as a simulated form in contrast to the real world of warfare. Nonetheless, warfare, also ritualized and rule bound in many of its incarnations, can be close kin to its simulated brethren, to the extent that—at times—it may be hard to assign a practice definitely to one category or another.

TABLETOP GAMES

While some of the earliest board games have left suggestive material traces without a rule book to guide our precise understanding, ancient games of strategy such as the Chinese *weiqi* (commonly known by its Japanese name, go), chess (derived from the Indian *chaturanga*), and their kin have evolved over the course of millennia and are still popular today. In such games, a defined field of conflict and a set of rules governing turn-based movement across this field provide the context for a battle between two opposing forces. Moving across a gridded board or map, players seek to incapacitate their opponent, encircling opposing pieces or capturing and removing them from the board. Through these maneuvers, a panoply of wars—historical, mythic, potential, and metaphoric—have been imaginatively played out.

In the example of go, there is evidence suggesting a long history of military use in China and elsewhere in Asia, where the game was cast as an example of, and a preparation for, the art of war itself (Halter 20). Chess, though it too was long understood through allegories of battle, takes on an explicitly militarized purpose only in the sixteenth and seventeenth centuries (Peterson, "Game" 4). As war in Europe became more regimented and rule bound, new versions of chess evolved to support the training of noblemen as would-be military officers. The principles of chess were understood in this context to carry over in direct and specific ways to the waging of war, increasingly understood in the Age of Reason as a precise, rational, and scientific undertaking. By the late eighteenth century, capitalizing on advances in cartography, the original chessboard expanded to include a vast grid representing real-world territory, over which thousands of infantry, cavalry, and artillery would do battle, accompanied by logistical pieces representing bridges, roads, fortifications, wagon convoys, supply magazines, and field bakeries (Halter 38). The board was no longer an undifferentiated grid but took on the properties of varied terrain designated by differently colored squares. In this development of "war chess" toward a more detailed rendering of the space of the battlefield we can recognize the modern impulse toward realist representation, which the writer Jorge Luis Borges described centuries later as a fantasy of the seventeenth century itself: the notion of a map so exacting and precise that it covers the entire breadth of the territory it seeks to represent ("On Exactitude in Science").

The most significant form of militarized chess is the Prussian war game, or *kriegsspiel*, developed in the early nineteenth century. The game was played with red and blue counters across gridded maps of real-world landscapes. Among its key innovations were the use of a referee to interpret and execute orders and adjudicate impacts and the incorporation of the randomizing function of a die alongside the use of probabilities derived from real-world data: all elements designed to replicate more closely the execution of battle from the perspective of commanding officers. Striving for a new level of realism by employing data derived from military history and experiment, *kriegsspiel* was embraced as an efficacious and enjoyable mode of training by the German military. By the closing decades of the century, in the face of Prussian military victories of the 1860s and 1870s, other European powers as well as Japan began to institute war gaming as military training. With counters representing units of varying sizes, topographical maps drawn to scale, and a time-limited window in which to undertake actions whose impact was gauged based on real-world experience, *kriegsspiel* represented a novel form of war simulation. The incorporation of ever more detailed data was often in conflict with playability, however, leading to a "free" variant, in which a human umpire replaced extensive rule books. Modified versions of the game, in which squares are replaced with hexagons to allow for more flexible movement, are still played today in both military and recreational contexts.

In the United States, war games were introduced in the closing decades of the nineteenth century, initially at the Naval War College and eventually spreading to other branches of the military. These "military simulations" (a nomenclature that deemphasizes the linkage between war and play) continue to be an important way in which the military evaluates, plans, and trains for future wars. In a testament to the enduring influence of *kriegsspiel*, opposing forces are still coded as blue (for the "home" team, from the original Prussian blue) and red. As the games developed to account for a wider range of factors—including weather, supply availability, and troop morale and exhaustion, alongside troop movements, ballistics, and geography—they required increasingly extensive feats of number crunching. As the data exceeded the capacity of human calculators, war gaming eventually conditioned the development of computer-assisted and fully computerized simulations.

Often played in combination with other modes of simulation, tabletop games have been granted an influential role by their relative economy, flexibility, and accessibility. At the Naval War College, hundreds of games were played in the interwar years, many focused on a possible war with Japan (Perla). In conflicts from Vietnam to the war in Iraq, gaming scenarios have often uncannily anticipated the unfolding of real-world military violence, raising complex questions about the function and impact of simulation. The Navy has continued to take a lead in this realm, as in the Global War Games, in which officers from all branches of the military, government officials, academics, industry representatives, and international personnel have all taken part. In addition, a politico-military variant of war gaming, in which economic and diplomatic variables are included in the calculations, has served in the training of officers, analysts, and policy makers at war colleges, government institutions such as the Pentagon and the State Department, and influential think tanks such as the RAND corporation.

In a civilian context, war games (sometimes referred to as "wargames" to distinguish from their militarized cousins) entered into mass production in the United States in the mid-twentieth century. Picking up steam across the 1960s, commercial tabletop games by innovators such as Avalon Hill and Simulations Publication, Inc. (SPI) established a thriving hobby market for wargaming, with hundreds of titles available by the late 1970s. Game titles and personnel often shifted between recreational and military contexts and, eventually, from analog to digital ones. By 1980, the president of SPI, James F. Dunnigan, was being called in by the Department of Defense to help design a nuclear-war game for military training purposes, and modified commercial games were sometimes adopted by the military (early examples of the flow between commercial and military gaming that will be discussed further in chapter 3). Game designers considered these modified versions less realistic than their commercial kin, to the extent they emphasized mathematical modeling over military history—increasing predictability and minimizing the more elusive elements of war—and involved data inputs shaped by contemporary political priorities and concerns.

Many of the most popular titles were designed around historical battles, such as *Gettysburg* (Avalon Hill, 1958), the inaugural entry of its type, which introduced into commercial gaming the hexagonal map that became standard in subsequent releases. Many more historical titles followed, games that put a premium on the notion of historical authenticity, supported by extensive research. Though their popularity peaked in the 1970s, a game such as *Desert Shield* (Victory Games), released in the fall of 1990, could still sell out just weeks after it hit the shelves. The game's success testifies to the popular appeal of gaming contemporary conflicts, or even future ones, alongside historical battles. In addition to these hobby games, mass-market titles such as *Risk* (Parker Brothers, 1959),

Stratego (Milton Bradley, 1961), *Battleship* (Milton Bradley, 1967), and *Axis and Allies* (revised for a popular market by Milton Bradley in 1983) have had enduring success, sharing shelf space with such venerable classics as *Life* (Milton Bradley, 1860) and *Monopoly* (Parker Brothers, 1935) and bringing some of the basic structures and principles of wargaming to a youth audience.

During the Cold War, when the threat of mass nuclear annihilation loomed as the face of contemporary conflict and noncombatants emerged as targets in newly explicit ways, engaging with fantasies of battles bounded by their own historical completion and reimagined through the perspective of a commanding officer may have proved particularly appealing. The orderly massing of troops across a circumscribed field of battle looked nothing like the imagination of nuclear holocaust, which developed simultaneous to the growing popularity of wargames. Wargames, with their heavy reliance on scientific data and probabilistic calculation, seek to map what they also recognize as unmappable. Despite efforts to incorporate something of the fog and friction of war into the structures of gameplay—by limiting the information available to any one side, for instance, and introducing randomizing elements such as the die—the complexities of war on the ground elude this mode of representation (as, indeed, they elude the simulations across this book).

Nonetheless, in the context of the nuclear age, wargames offer the fantasy of a relatively ordered and contained form of violence, with outcomes that can be anticipated and impacts that can be measured.

Not all conflicts are gamed with the same consistency, however. "Irregular warfare" is rarely gamed, though as a mode of armed conflict including guerrilla wars, internal wars, and counterinsurgencies, it has been by far the most widespread since the end of World War II (Train and Ruhnke 515). Instead, "conventional wars" of the nineteenth and twentieth centuries (including the Napoleonic Wars, the U.S. Civil War, and World Wars I and II) serve as the primary setting for popular wargames. Gamers put a high premium on issues of real-world correspondence, working to bring gameplay into line with historical facts and real-world variables. Nonetheless, certain aspects of war remain largely outside the orbit of conventional gaming, including ethnic cleansings, genocide, and terrorism. This editing of the historical record in the context of an overarching concern with authenticity resonates with the war reenactments discussed later in this chapter, in which, for instance, Nazi "impressions" based on the snappy uniforms of German soldiers are very popular, though reenactors insist these carry no particular ideological baggage (Thompson 68). To the extent that realistic representation is a central feature in the promotion of wargames—and to the extent that these games help to shape the cultural imagination of what "real" war is—these emphases and omissions are significant to consider.

Gameplay also links up to the construction and performance of masculinity in ways worth briefly noting. Tabletop games encourage the amassing of detailed factual and technical knowledge, for instance, a trait they hold in common with other forms of wargaming such as battle reenactments and videogames. This encyclopedic impulse relates to a drive toward mastery conventionally held as a masculine ideal. In addition, the commanding-eye view of traditional games constructs a gendered position of control, even as the fantasies of violence that gameplay engages may undermine this sense of control: a tension central to the pleasures of gameplay itself.

Vietnam exerted particular kinds of pressures on the simulation of war, however, and across the 1960s gameplay began to shift. In contrast to large-scale strategic games focused on entire conflicts unfolding across months or even years of gametime, new tactical games emerged focused on smaller units and shorter increments of time in the context of a single engagement. While the player is still in a position of control, this narrowing focus resonates with ascendant modes of warfare in which small groups of men operate at a relative remove from central command. Thus, while the unraveling of clear martial and moral objectives in the context of Vietnam may have encouraged the market for nostalgic modes of gameplay on the one hand, the war also conditioned a broader cultural shift toward the individual soldier as a focus of attention and identification (a shift we will consider further in chapter 2).

The trendsetting *Dungeons and Dragons* (Tactical Studies Rules, 1974) developed out of these varied traditions, constructing a fantastical rather than a historical or future war and drawing inspiration from early precedents such as *kriegsspiel* (as well as from Tolkien's *Lord of the Rings* trilogy, released in paperback in the United States in the mid-1960s). The massive success of the game inaugurated role-playing as an influential new genre, one that represented a significant break with wargaming traditions even as it built on and carried them forward. *Dungeon and Dragons* took the shrinking focus of wargames down to a single in-game character, relinquishing the broader position of command for a more developed identification between player and character. This more focused mode of identification was cemented through a more expansive sense of agency within the gameworld, as players could direct their characters to undertake an unprecedented variety of actions, "simulat[ing] the experience of being a person who did many things other than commanding" (Peterson, "Game" 23).

While the success of *Dungeons and Dragons* sparked a new market in fantasy games, traditional wargames focusing on historical realism persisted. And while the emergence of role-playing as a popular genre shifted the mode of identification with gameworlds and characters, campaign and conflict-level games simulating battle on a massive scale continued to be released as well. All of these trends—strategic and tactical games focused on positions of command, as well as role-playing games pivoting on a heightened sense of agency and identification—endured into the digital age. In simulating the experience of war through an emphasis on the properties of real spaces and weapons, offering a commander's-eye view as well as a focus on individual combatants, and highlighting the appeal of role-playing, tabletop games represent one meaningful history of the videogames to come. These games have enjoyed a popular resurgence in recent years, fueled by independent designers, crowdfunding structures, and the enthusiastic embrace of videogamers themselves (Wingfield; Jolin).

GAMING IN MINIATURE

The incorporation of miniature figures in role-playing games such as *Dungeons and Dragons* derives from another popular mode of playing at war: the enduring institution of toy soldiers. While the production of martial figurines has much deeper roots, playing with toy soldiers was introduced as an aristocratic pastime in the sixteenth century, alongside the growth of modern armies. Toy soldiers increased in popularity in subsequent centuries, as cheaper tin versions and eventually mass-produced and hollow-cast ones made them available to a burgeoning middle (and eventually even to a working) class. In Britain, the cross-class "toy soldier craze" of the late nineteenth and early twentieth centuries constituted one prominent aspect of the increasingly militarized national culture that helped to condition vigorous, voluntary military enlistment after the outbreak of World War I (K. Brown).

As a form, miniature soldiers lend themselves both to the restaging of historical battles and to more fluid forms of play, though they have often been released in sets organized around specific conflicts and complete with appropriately outfitted figurines. Toy weapons too are often historically specific, as in the example of the Modern Trench Warfare set of 1917, which came complete with a trench shovel, grenade thrower, and sandbags for barricades (Halter 53). (An earlier "exploding trench" that spring-launched its occupants with a sharp bang was apparently quickly withdrawn; Peterson, *Playing* 270.) As toy soldiers developed across the twentieth century, they acquired moving parts and action-oriented stances, typified by G.I. Joe, America's Movable Fighting Man, released by Hasbro in 1964 in Action Soldier, Sailor, Pilot, and Marine versions (with accessory sets available separately). Plastic cowboys and Indians (which come to this day colored blue and red) fall into this miniature gaming history as well, which points us toward other kinds of playground games—and the histories of colonialism and imperialism they rehearse—as well as toward the popular battle reenactments of the Wild West show, discussed later in this chapter.

Present-day battle reenactors often half jokingly attribute their zealous pursuit of war games to an abundant love of toy soldiers in their youth (and scholars offer more straight-faced evaluations of the connections between such childhood play and later endorsement of military values and perspectives). But simulating war with miniature troops has long been a popular pastime with grown men as well. The British writer H. G. Wells staged elaborate battles on his lawn, for instance, and published two short books on playing war in miniature in the decade before World War I. While the first, *Floor Wars* (1911), was focused on toy soldiers as a source of children's play, the second, *Little Wars* (1913), famously details "a game for boys from twelve years of age to one hundred and fifty and for that more intelligent sort of girl who likes boys' games and books." This second book helped spur the growth of miniature wargaming as a hobby that continues to this day.

Another very different landmark in the cultural history of military miniatures is the elaborate World War II dioramas of the American designer Norman Bel Geddes. Bel Geddes (an early wargamer himself) was commissioned by *Life* magazine to create scale models of recent battles and potential future operations. Photographs of the models appeared in *Life* across the early 1940s, presenting the American public with an image of war that was both highly stylized and, in its detailed renderings of hardware and topographies, strikingly realistic (Ramirez; a very cinematic conjunction, as we will see in chapter 2). The models and photographs were also displayed at the Museum of Modern Art in 1944, in an exhibition inspired by the Army's and Navy's interest in their significance as training aids (Grischkowsky). Both miniaturize the violence from an aerial perspective far removed from the action below, aligned with the position of a mythic pilot in some instances and a more abstract god's-eye view in others. Thus, in the pages of *Life* and the galleries of the Museum of Modern Art, Bel Geddes's work invited viewers to imagine themselves within—but also largely above—the contemporary mise-en-scène of war. More recent works, such as David Levinthal's photographic reproductions of miniature war scenes or Brian Conley's *Miniature War in Iraq* installations, suggest the ongoing if paradoxical impulse to immerse through mechanisms of miniaturization (Levinthal; Conley).

In parallel with other tabletop games though on a lesser scale, miniature wargaming in the United States reached a popular audience in the 1950s. Staging historical battles on carefully sculpted sand tables or elaborate handmade dioramas, miniature wargames mix historical accuracy with the vicissitudes of a die-driven game. These games evince a strong investment in notions of authenticity and the real, both in their modeling of accurate weapons, uniforms, and topographies and through their exacting calculations of ballistics, the impediments of weather and terrain, and troop fatigue and injury. Like other tabletop games, miniature wargames model the violence of history on a manageable scale, placing players in positions of command and control. Wells's own nostalgic inclinations—he eschewed modern technologies such as railroads and rifles in favor of a resolutely dated imagination of battle—may have helped to establish this orientation. At the same time, miniature games, in the interests of realism and again like their tabletop cousins, introduce through the roll of the die something of the unpredictable "friction" of combat. In this, the games engage a form of play not beholden to the historical record, even as they invest themselves heavily in the simulation of specific historical settings and scenarios (a conjunction familiar from multiplayer online games today).

Miniature war provides a link between the more abstract tabletop games discussed earlier and the battle reenactments discussed shortly. In contrast to games played out on grids and paper, toy soldiers simulate war through realistically embodied figures, emphasizing the appeal of authentic weapons and uniforms and imaginatively mapping out the movements of troops "on the ground." Gamers speak of the "magic circle" they enter when immersed in these miniature worlds, "in which the diorama comes alive with all the stress, elation, calculation, exhaustion, and uncertainty of combat" (Conley 409). This notion of a space set apart from everyday life, in which the simulated battle temporarily overwhelms the space and time of the "real" world, resonates suggestively with the experience of a "period rush" described by live battle reenactors. As both these examples suggest, the realism of these simulations may be supported by the authenticity of props and scenarios but is ultimately focused more on the subjective experience of the players themselves (an insight with relevance for screen-based simulations as well).

Contemporary wargamers, like Wells before them, sometimes highlight the pacifistic impulse of playing at war, suggesting that hobby wargaming helps to ward off the real thing by emphasizing its ultimate futility. Now as in the past, however, these forms of simulated war generate controversy, alternately claimed as patriotic, pedagogic, memorializing, or bellicose. In establishing war simulation as a popular pastime, through which consumers play at historical or ongoing conflicts or rehearse future ones, tabletop games and miniatures represent a meaningful lineage with the culture of militainment today, to which we return in chapter 3.

COMBAT AND CONTACT SPORTS

Historically, both the benefits and the limitations of tabletop games have been associated with their abstraction from the embodied experience of war. While their remove from the field of combat has allowed for their use as intellectual tools of military training and planning, in recreational contexts, this distance has sometimes opened them to scorn, as in early representations of chess as the pastime of men too indolent or carefree to take up more active pursuits (Halter 33). Abstracted and miniaturized, these games offer a fantasy of control divorced from lived experience. In this, they contrast with modes of simulation that emphasize knowledge and understanding as available only through visceral identification with the embodied experience of war. While the narrowing focus of tabletop games in the 1960s and emergence of role-playing games in the 1970s offer a closer identification with the agency (and injury) of individual figures, important distinctions remain between tabletop gaming and traditions such as sports and battle reenactments.

In the history of combat and contact sports, we witness a different kind of simulation, one that puts a premium on intense, embodied experience. While games such as chess and *kriegsspiel* limit the risk and anxiety of combat action to focus on large-scale questions of strategy, sports highlight the experience of strenuous physical effort, violence, and risk on the ground. Like the tabletop games discussed earlier, across epochs and cultures, combat and contact sports have often been imagined in relationship to war, serving as preparation and training as well as a form of martial display. At the same time, they have functioned as popular entertainment spectacles, pivoting around the tension between deadly violence and recreative pleasure that has long marked the terrain of war simulation.

The example of gladiatorial combat in ancient Rome highlights this spectacular element, as fights were organized explicitly as a form of entertainment and commemoration, at first in the context of private leisure and subsequently for the public, in arenas and amphitheaters equipped to hold tens of thousands. While many fights pitted one gladiator against another, others featured entire armies—or even navies, on artificial lakes constructed for this purpose—in contests staged as reenactments of famous historical battles. Though these contests were presented as bloody entertainment spectacles quite distinct from the actual practice of war, gladiatorial training provided a model for the training of soldiers, and like soldiers, gladiators—though slaves—were prized on the basis of their perceived courage and fighting ability (Van Creveld 66–68).

Medieval tournaments present another historical example of a combat sport that mirrored war while providing a popular entertainment spectacle. Here, opposing cavalry units charged one another with lance, axe, or sword, engaging in bloody "mock" battles. Originating in France and spreading from there, the tournaments offered opportunities for the display of martial prowess and for commercial gain, as well as providing a theatrical spectacle. Though most tournaments involved hundreds rather than thousands of knights, the largest is reported to have engaged as many as twenty thousand men (Van Creveld 115).

Particularly interesting for our purposes, later more formally structured jousting matches often included the addition of fantastical elements (damsels, dragons, and unicorns featured frequently) to increase pleasure and interest in the spectacle of combat. Knights in these contests sometimes competed under the guise of legendary or historical figures. The introduction of heroic scenarios from the genre of medieval romance suggests the way narrative traditions can come to structure the excitement and appeal of simulated war, granting significance to the spectacle of combat by embedding it within familiar story forms. Medieval tournaments later became the subject of reenactments of their own, as in the 1839 Elginton Tournament in Scotland—attended by 150,000 spectators following preparations that consumed the better part of a year—and have continued so to this day; the Elginton Tournament itself, partially rained out in the nineteenth century, was restaged in 1989, offering the spectacular reenactment of a reenactment of simulated combat (Van Creveld 217).

In the context of the United States, football has been compared to a gladiatorial contest in its staging of an often brutal physical conflict before energetically approving masses (and team monikers and mascots across the country suggest the ongoing function of gladiators as a source of inspiration). While the prevalence of fatalities in early football has given way to more gradual kinds of injury and bodily trauma, the game has long been defined through both its violence and its status as a mass entertainment spectacle. In contrast to the gladiatorial contests, however, which maintained a distinction between the slaves who fought in the arena and the men who soldiered in the battlefield, football was historically conceptualized as a form of simulated battle that might provide young men with opportunities for discipline and strenuous effort in the absence of a war to fight.

During the period of football's rise at the end of the nineteenth century, there was much concern over the "softening" of Anglo-American middle-class men. Manly and martial virtues were understood in this context to depend on the vigorous pursuit of "the strenuous life," defined by activities that emphasized physicality and muscularity alongside bodily risk (Eagle). By staging controlled combat in the form of a game, football was believed to instill habits germane to an ascendant world of business (including discipline, hard work, and efficient, coordinated efforts within a hierarchical structure of command) while inoculating middle-class men against the softening that business itself was feared to induce. Like the experience of combat, the transformative potential of football—its ability to turn boys into men—was imagined to reside in bodily suffering and risk, as well as muscular strength and physical vigor. Fraternal organizations such as the Boy Scouts emerged in this same period out of similar impulses, offering up other opportunities for simulated soldiering in an effort to raise up a generation of fit and vigorous Anglo-American men, those subjects presumed to represent the political and economic fortunes of the nation. Today, organizations such as the Young Marines, Junior ROTC, the Homeland Security Office's Explorer Program, and others carry on in the tradition of simulated soldiering as training for young Americans.

One early illustration of the link between the field of battle and the playing field appears in Stephen Crane's Civil War novel *The Red Badge of Courage* (published as a book in 1895). Considered one of the most realistic fictional accounts of war, the novel describes the movements of soldiers in battle as if describing a football game, a suggestive (if anachronistic) reversal of the combat metaphors through which football itself was depicted at the end of the nineteenth century. A few year later, war correspondents such as Richard Harding Davis and Crane himself would report on the Spanish-American War in similar terms. The connection hinges on the nationalist conviction that football, like war, provides an exciting opportunity to cheer on the "home" team and the notion that risky, physically intense experience harbors a rejuvenating potential for the national as for the individual (male) body. The endurance of this linkage is suggested in the visual and rhetorical conventions that continue to flow between football and war a century later, in which—both live and on television—games are interlaced with martial displays, and war is produced by the media through the conventions of prime-time sporting events.

Games such as paintball also highlight the merger of sports and simulated combat. Originally called the National Survival Game and first played in the woods of New England, paintball was initially imagined apart from explicit combat scenarios. But as the popularity of paintball spread across the 1980s, influenced by screen-based war fantasies such as *Rambo*, the sport took a militarized turn. Commercial playing fields were constructed to replicate theme-park-style battlefields in Vietnam and Central America. That one such location—the Sat Cong Village outside of Los Angeles—also provided a shooting location for the film *Platoon* suggestively highlights the relationship of Hollywood to the sport's appeal (Gibson 127). Now called simply SC Village, the one-hundred-acre site ("World Famous since 1984") offers paintball, airsoft, and "paintball 4 kids" on twenty-five different fields named for sites around the world, including China Beach, the Mekong Delta, Bosnia, Kosovo, Baghdad, and Fallujah, providing stage sets on which to play out the fantasy of combat, both historical and contemporary.

As a popular form of militarized play and a wide-spread competitive sport, paintball in the 1980s sought to produce virtual veterans through the simulated experience of combat. As the sociologist James Gibson argues, it "offered men the opportunity to participate in a film-fantasy world rather than just to watch it" (127). Playing fields complete with mock tanks and helicopters and increasingly militarized magazine-fed paintball guns, as well as the more realistic airsoft guns also used for military training, highlight the sport's status as simulated combat, "as close as you can get to the real thing." As paintball increased in popularity, choosing a "persona" and costuming oneself accordingly greatly augmented the combat fantasy, providing an important aspect of the sport's appeal and suggesting a connection with both videogames and the battle reenactments discussed in the next section.

Laser tag provides an even more direct link between recreational and military modes of gaming. Emerging around the same time as paintball and, like paintball, rehearsing some basic military tactics in its gameplay, laser tag expanded quickly from its original recreational context to emerge as a form of military training. Pairing weapon-mounted lasers with receptor-laden vests, helmets, and vehicles, the military's Multiple Integrated Laser Engagement System (MILES) augmented the combat realism of massive field exercises such as those undertaken at the National Training Center (NTC) in

California's Mojave Desert, one example of the military maneuvers to which we now turn.

MILITARY MANEUVERS

The practice of simulating war through reenacted battle extends across decades and contexts, operating as a form of military training, a kind of geopolitical theater, a popular entertainment spectacle, a recreational pastime, and—of course—a central aspect of the making of war movies. These contexts differ in many ways, though they share some underlying investments. Battle reenactments are underwritten by the conviction that to know war—to understand or prepare for it—it is necessary to experience it in an embodied way. This conviction is coupled with the belief that, while nothing can replicate the actual experience of war, it is nonetheless possible to meaningfully simulate the experience of battle. In modern reenactments of historical conflicts, the issue of authenticity is central to how the meaning and merit of these battle simulations are evaluated.

In the context of military training, large-scale reenactments—known as field exercises or maneuvers—can involve tens or even hundreds of thousands of troops and extend across vast areas of land, sea, and sky, all around the globe. The authenticity of these simulations is understood as essential to their efficacy, and the effort to reproduce combat action in realistic ways has been an elaborate and expensive one, which draws heavily on the techniques of stage and screen to create compelling and immersive spaces and experiences. Weapons, terrain, and tactics must replicate the anticipated conditions of warfare as thoroughly as possible, and troops themselves must be released from other obligations to participate. Among other aims, these exercises seek to simulate the physical deprivations and discomforts of war that elude the modes of gaming discussed earlier—the punishing weight of packs, the lack of sleep, the extremes of heat, cold, thirst, and hunger (an impulse they share with civilian reenactments).

Field exercises became a regular form of military training in the eighteenth century, making use of large standing armies that had not been a feature of social and military organization since the fall of the Roman Empire. These maneuvers could last for weeks and involve thousands of troops, yet more than simulations of actual combat, they served as elaborate and extended drills. Two-sided simulations emerged in the nineteenth century, facilitated by the new technology of the railroad that enabled the mass transportation of troops and supplies

(Van Creveld 191). By the last decade of that century, every major army was holding some form of simulated battle as a means of military training.

By the early twentieth century, maneuvers had developed into massive undertakings often attended by large numbers of spectators, including official dignitaries, the press, and the general public. In addition to their training purposes, these maneuvers served to test new technologies of communication and transport. In England in the late 1920s, for instance, on a large tract of training ground on the Salisbury Plain, the newly formed Experimental Mechanical Force—the first fully mechanized and motorized force in history—fought against conventional infantry and cavalry in a series of simulated battles destined to revolutionize modern warfare. Thousands of spectators traveled to Salisbury Plain to watch the parade of new technology, which included armored cars, tanks, motorized artillery, infantry in trucks and half-tracks, and the occasional motorcycle. The maneuvers of this mobile, mechanized force were accompanied by other attractions, including military bands, trick riding, and a display of "illuminated aeroplanes," to constitute a full and varied program (Der Derian 26), highlighting the double function of such exercises as training and spectacle.

In the United States, field exercises remained relatively small through the first half of the twentieth century, although this changed with the Louisiana Maneuvers of 1940 and 1941, initiated as the war in Europe raged. The Maneuvers witnessed the field testing of new weapons, tactics, leadership, and organization for an Army that had changed little since the end of World War I. While the exercises of 1940 mobilized seventy thousand troops—including the first armored division in U.S. history—in the more comprehensive exercises of 1941, which extended over two three-week periods, almost half a million men fought across thirty-four hundred square miles of sparsely populated marshland, pine forest, rivers, and swamps, in what *Life* magazine called "the greatest sham battle in U.S. history" (M. Perry). The assembled force included two armored divisions, attack and dive bombers, spotter and reconnaissance planes, and troop transports. To create a more immersive environment, sounds of battle were piped in on loudspeakers, canisters of smoke enveloped the battlefield, and bags of white sand were dropped from above to simulate the impact of artillery shells; millions of blanks and hundreds of thousands of antitank rounds were allocated (M. Perry). Many of the commanders distinguishing themselves during the maneuvers soon assumed leadership roles in the war, including Lieutenant Colonel Dwight D. Eisenhower. In the 1990s, the modern Louisiana Maneuvers referenced the significance of the original exercises while underscoring a difference: neither maneuvers nor in Louisiana, they employed new simulation technologies to replace the massing of boots on the ground and the massive expense of getting them there (J. Brown).

Major maneuvers continued after the war, involving troops stationed around the globe, in training exercises that doubled as a form of "perception management": advertisements for U.S. military force and readiness. Such exercises include Team Spirit, inaugurated in 1976, in which a simulated North Korean invasion was repelled by combined U.S. and South Korean forces. While the exercise was officially suspended in 1993, joint military maneuvers involving tens of thousands of troops have continued since on the Korean Peninsula, with the stated aim of enhancing readiness and maintaining regional stability, purposes for which the performative aspect of these exercises—which establishes readiness through gestures of readying—is central. Other joint maneuvers, such as the massive Reforger exercise held annually in Germany throughout the Cold War, attest to the vast scale of simulated combat, deploying tens of thousands of troops for price tags topping $50 million. The staging of mock battles as a massive, costly form of political theater is evident more recently in the joint exercises launched by Russia on September 11, 2018, in which three thousand Chinese troops joined three hundred thousand Russian forces for games billed as the largest of the post-Soviet era (Troianovski, Fifield, and Stone).

In a stateside example, the Navy/Marine "experiment" Kernel Blitz 99 welcomed an unusually high degree of media coverage during the war in Kosovo under the assumption that "information can be a good deterrent" (T. Perry). The exercise included helicopter raids, amphibious landings, land and air strikes, and a hospital ship supplied with five hundred mock casualties (simulated for maximum realism with help from Hollywood makeup artists). In the experiment's Urban Warrior component—which took place in the San Francisco Bay Area in March 1999 and included an earthquake, a terrorist attack, and a civil uprising—a combined force of six thousand Marines and seven hundred sailors, with the support of three hundred civilian reenactors, played out a collection of scenarios designed to prepare for military operations in urban terrain (MOUT) (Der Derian 124). Tricked out with the latest high-tech gear, as well as low-tech weapons such as sledgehammers and axes, the urban warriors attracted an audience of both spectators and protestors.

More recent exercises include the Rim of the Pacific Exercise (RIMPAC), the largest international maritime exercise, administered biennially by the U.S. Navy's Pacific Fleet headquartered at Pearl Harbor. In 2018,

RIMPAC featured twenty-five thousand personnel from twenty-five different nations (though its culminating event on Oahu—an amphibious assault on an airfield, involving thousands of ground, air, and maritime forces—attracted only an invited audience of media and military families; Shikina). The film *Battleship* (dir. Berg, 2012), based on the board game of the same name, takes as its setting the 2012 RIMPAC, offering an example of the tangled imagination of different modes of war gaming across live and screen-based, military and civilian contexts.

Simulated air war likewise functions as a training exercise, a show of military power in the context of international conflicts, and a popular entertainment spectacle for civilian audiences. During the Vietnam War, the U.S. Navy Fighter Weapons School (popularly known as Topgun) launched an aerial combat training program in preparation for potential air war against the Soviet Union. In the post-Vietnam era, the Air Force Fighter Weapons School at Nellis Air Force Base inaugurated its Red Flag exercise, which engages U.S. and allied pilots from around the world in "realistic combat scenarios" in which Red battles Blue above the fifteen-thousand-square-mile Nevada Test and Training Range. The mock battles of the Fighter Weapons Schools have been both popular live attractions and the subject of cinematic reenactments, as in *Red Flag: The Ultimate Game* (dir. Taylor, 1981), *Top Gun* (dir. Scott, 1986), and the more recent IMAX documentary *Fighter Pilot: Operation Red Flag* (dir. Low, 2004) (though a statement on the Nellis Air Force Base website that "many communities in southern Nevada see and hear Nellis aircraft 24 hours a day, seven days a week" suggests that all civilian audiences may not be voluntary ones; "Exercises"). In addition to these exercises, air shows have long been a staple of militarized cultural attractions and often include reenactments of well-known battles.

The Red Flag exercises traditionally focused on air-to-air combat scenarios, employing only simulated ground forces. While some people criticize these scenarios as obsolete, the exercise has evolved since 2001 to incorporate new threats, including those concentrated in the desert outpost of Gotham City, a town of painted shipping containers on which simulated bombs are dropped (or "placed") (Magnuson). Green Flag meanwhile (formerly Air Warrior) involves Army, Navy, Air Force, and Marines, alongside allied air forces, in a massive joint ground-air exercise (one that expends over seven hundred pounds of live and training ordnance; Nellis Air Force Base, "Green").

Green Flag West takes place at the National Training Center at Fort Irwin, forty miles northeast of Barstow, California, which hosts "the most technologically advanced and elaborate training facilities in the world" (NTC and Fort Irwin). Here, "with an assist from Disneyland, Hollywood, and Silicon Valley," the desert supplies a theatrical "backdrop for the melodrama of national security" (Der Derian 19). Fort Irwin is located on land originally established by President Franklin Roosevelt as the Mojave Anti-Aircraft Range and later used as a training center during the Korean and Vietnam Wars. Now the site of the NTC, troops from all services spend twenty-one-day rotations here, participating in simulated combat scenarios prior to deployment overseas. The NTC emphasizes its simulations as both tough and realistic, effective to the extent that they are—like the desert terrain—"unforgiving"; field exercises endeavor to produce for trainees the "worst day ever" (NTC and Fort Irwin). In a lavish bid for authenticity, troops train with their own equipment, including tanks and helicopters transported to the Mojave Desert at great expense. At Fort Irwin as at other training locations, a resident regiment enacts the opposing force (OPFOR) across a variety of engagements, serving as both the enemy and the home team, with all the attendant advantages of the latter. As a result, OPFOR is almost impossible to beat (Van Creveld 215).

Simulations are staged in the Box, short for the sandbox, a term that recalls at once the sand tables of miniature wargaming and the arid desert landscape that constitutes the Fort's one thousand acres of mock cities, battle arenas, gunnery ranges, and airfields, as well as a vast network of underground tunnels and caves (Manaugh and Twilley). The Box has been the site of many firsts, including the rollout of MILES. It was also home to the first MOUT exercises, and after the Black Hawk down incident in Mogadishu in 1993, training at the site shifted toward urban combat scenarios in mock villages like the Afghan Ertebat Shar (originally known as the Iraqi Medina Wasl; Manaugh and Twilley). Like Gotham City, the village is constructed of shipping containers, here dressed up to suggest a vaguely Middle Eastern location. Like the paintball fields of SC Village on a much-grander scale, the set includes a dusty main street and surrounding buildings, sparsely ornamented with a few objects to connote its fictional locale. In contrast to the eerily empty streets of SC Village, however, here the town is populated with Afghan-speaking "locals," both friendly and threatening, with whom trainees must interact: some of the hundreds of civilian role-players (many of Middle Eastern descent) hired by the Army to populate Fort Irwin's mock villages and augment the realism of its simulations. In a suggestive link between training simulations and their mass-mediated cousins, audio engineers for the reboot of the popular videogame *Medal of Honor* (Electronic Arts, 2010) used Medina Wasl to record the weapons fire, exploding targets, and Apache helicopters that constitute the game's "authentic" sounds of battle (Suellentrop).

Combat simulations at Fort Irwin double as a civilian entertainment spectacle, the highlight of a tour that includes a briefing and short film, lunch, and a visit to the Box (as well as to the gift shop). Visitors are encouraged to bring their cameras and take pictures to share on social media as they wander through Ertebat Shar while reenactors attempt to sell them fake loaves of bread, fruit, and plastic slabs of meat (Manaugh and Twilley). After their stroll, visitors take up posts above the street to witness the main attraction of an action-packed live exercise as it plays out on the Hollywood-style stage set below, complete with pyrotechnic effects and simulated casualties, including sucking chest wounds and loss of limb (the latter reenacted by amputees hired for this purpose). For maneuvers such as those at Fort Irwin, the Army trains soldiers specifically in the application of realistic simulated wounds (Hernandez; another area of overlap between Hollywood and the military). The sense of being on a film set is heightened by the presence of cameras, as (in addition to the ubiquitous cell phones) the simulations are extensively filmed by the military for later replay and analysis.

Attractions such as the Army's annual All American Week at Fort Bragg in North Carolina deliver theatrical spectacle to a popular audience more directly. Without the conceit of a training exercise, All American Week presents a massive show of military hard- and software, including in 2018 nearly eight hundred paratroopers alighting from cargo planes one thousand feet up, fifteen thousand soldiers marching out of the mist (simulating the smoke used to obscure troop movements in battle), the "buzzing" of the crowd with Black Hawk and Apache helicopters, live firing of long-range artillery rockets, and a mock battle including the blowing up of a building and killing of insurgents. Before this vast military spectacle, an appreciative crowd gathers in the thousands, drawn by the promise of seeing "the real thing" (Cooper). This practice of reenacting battle as an entertainment spectacle has deep roots: we might think of the Roman gladiators, whom the soldiers at Fort Bragg imitate in a competition to display their "warriorlike skills" (Cooper).

RECREATIONAL REENACTMENTS

For crowds gathered on hilltops and rooftops, in fields and arenas, and before their television and computer screens, both live battles and their simulations have long provided a popular attraction. During the U.S. Civil War, for instance, civilians flocked to battle sites alongside politicians and the press to witness history in the making, even if distance and obscured vision often revealed little more than smoke and the muffled sounds of musket and artillery fire (and even if, as at the First Battle of Bull Run, the shifting lines of battle might engulf spectators themselves). Spectators still gather to watch war in this way, as in the example of Israelis congregating on hilltops to watch (and applaud) the bombardment of Gaza (Mieszkowski, *War*). With televisual coverage of the Gulf War in 1991, spectating live war entered the mainstream of American culture, augmented today by online access to combat from around the world. While the impulses to watch live war, training exercises, or the reenactment of historical battles may differ, across these varied contexts war functions as a voyeuristic spectacle for people positioned outside the immediate reach of combat action.

In addition to classical examples such as the Roman reenactments, modern theatrical examples include the wildly popular sham battles at the center of Buffalo Bill's Wild West show, the most lucrative commercial entertainment of the late nineteenth and early twentieth centuries. Alongside its colorful parade of Rough Riders of the World and its showcasing of riding and shooting stunts, the Wild West featured melodramatic reenactments of mythic scenes from the Plains Wars—the stirring Attack on the Wagon Train, for instance, or the poignant Last Stand—as well as contemporary overseas exploits such as the Spanish-American and Philippine-American Wars. Despite the show's overt flamboyance, it staked its reputation on claims of realism and authenticity, highlighted by its shuttling of historical actors (including Buffalo Bill himself) back and forth between lived experience and its theatrical reenactment. The show traveled widely in the United States and Europe, inspiring attractions such as the Boer War exhibit at the Louisiana Purchase Exposition in 1904—billed as the "most realistic military spectacle known in the history of the world" (Fillis)—that included a fifteen-acre arena in which hundreds of British and Boer veterans would reenact major battles twice a day.

Whether at the Wild West show or Fort Irwin, battle reenactments place their spectators in a relatively passive position—thrilled and agitated by the action and violence but at the same time cordoned off from them. In contrast both to this position and to the commanding perspective constructed by tabletop games, the tradition of civilian battle reenactment strives to simulate war through the active, embodied experience of a soldier on the field. Like the military trainees for whom the efficacy of training relies on collapsing the distance between war and its simulation—the more closely an exercise resembles the experience of war, the more effective it is held to be—civilian reenactors seek to know war by replicating its physical and material realities as closely as they can, minus the crucial element of live fire. Instead of mastery (or perhaps alongside it), these war games seek to produce something of the chaotic, overwhelming, physically absorbing experience of combat itself.

Unlike the simulation of battle in the context of military training, which is largely accepted as necessary or even inevitable, civilian reenactments attract controversy alongside their often sizable and enthusiastic audiences. While field exercises signify the serious business of military preparedness, recreational reenactments are sometimes viewed as disrespectful or even disturbing, uncritical celebrations of violence that trivialize the real suffering and trauma of war. The reenactment of death and injury is taken to be in particularly poor taste in this context (though in the context of war films, we might note, it is the spectacle of simulated death and injury that provides the basis of a much-celebrated realism: a point to which we will return in chapter 2). Interestingly, those who disparage the practice of reenactment often liken it to the playing of cowboys and Indians—a charge that casts mock battles as juvenile though also, in its unwitting nod to the Wild West show, recalls one of the most influential progenitors of simulated battle as a mainstay of American popular entertainment.

Like tabletop games, recreational reenactments encompass a wide range of historical conflicts, including the Napoleonic Wars, the U.S. Revolutionary and Civil Wars, World Wars I and II, and, to a lesser extent, the Korean and Vietnam Wars. Though their origins are found in the veteran encampments, historical pageants, and artillery associations of the early twentieth century (Horwitz; Thompson; Turner, "Bloodless"), hobby reenacting emerged in the 1950s, contemporary with commercial tabletop games. It increased in size and popularity during the centennial Civil War commemorations of the 1960s, which included the restaging of significant battles. Spreading from Civil War reenactments to other conflicts, by the 1990s, tens of thousands of reenactors across the country were taking part in vast mock battles, in addition to smaller-scale skirmishes and encampments. The 125th anniversary reenactment of the Battle of Gettysburg in 1988, for instance, drew a reported ten thousand reenactors and even more spectators (Turner, "Play" 56); by 1998, the number of mock troops had increased to twenty-five thousand.

War reenactments fall into two broad categories organized around public or private events. Public events—often overtly commercialized—are larger and attract a sizable audience, including friends and family members, who participate alongside reenactors in the rituals of camp life. Private events—like public ones, generally scheduled over the course of a weekend—attract a more select crowd and focus on tactics rather than large-scale spectacles of battle. While authenticity is the gold standard across the hobby, private-event reenactors are focused with a particular intensity on accurately recreating the material and corporeal conditions of battle. They expend an extraordinary amount of time and money in pursuit of this goal, seeking out or tailoring for themselves meticulous reconstructions of period uniforms, gear, and everyday objects, down to the inside seams of jacket linings and the contents of their pockets. Attention to these kinds of details garners particular admiration among the reenactment community, suggesting that the most compelling indications of a "hard-core" reenactor (one committed to the idea of authenticity at all costs) may be those that are not readily visible. Authentic objects are not necessarily understood as original ones, however, as the patina of age undercuts rather than amplifies the claims of realistic simulation (Gapps 398; in the present day of World War II, for instance, a World War II uniform would not be moth-eaten or tattered). A thriving cottage industry has thus emerged to supply reenactors with uniforms, weapons, and other items, exactingly crafted to period specifications. In partial reward of these efforts, the most "authentic" of reenactors are frequently tapped as extras on film and television sets, bringing with them an adherence to period detail (as well as much of their own gear) (Gapps 402).

Though endlessly emphasized by reenactors, the concept of authenticity is in fact quite selective. It is often mobilized as a rationale for largely excluding women from the field of combat, for instance, and an African American soldier in a white World War I unit may be cast as a violation of the contemporary segregation of troops. While race and gender are policed through a discourse of authenticity, however, aspects of embodiment such as age and body type fall outside its purview (in violation of the historical record, Confederate reenactors may be both old and heavyset, for example, though gaunt ones are reckoned more hard-core): a discrepancy that highlights the function of the hobby in consolidating a martial identity defined as both white and male.

As with tabletop gaming, the reenactments are both constrained and open-ended. The mise-en-scène of battle is constructed with careful attention to realistic detail: when the Army Corps of Engineers volunteered to dig permanent trenches for a World War I reenactment group in exchange for use of the site for the training of special operations forces, for instance, the group rejected this proposal in part over uncertainty that the Army would dig the trenches properly (Thompson 43; highlighting the ongoing association of greater authenticity with recreational over military forms of war gaming). At the private events in particular, however, once the stage has been set and the costumes donned, there is little concern with adherence to any established historical script or predetermined course of action.

More than anything, authenticity in the context of the reenactments signifies the texture of embodied experience: the feel of a particular kind of cloth or weight of a particular rifle, the stab of hunger and the drag of fatigue, the cold and damp beneath you as you sleep. For hardcore reenactors, the courting of bodily suffering is paramount to achieving the desired experience of the "time warp" or "period rush" (Turner, "Bloodless"; Horwitz), in which the sensory fantasy of a historical past overwhelms the material realities of a here and now. Thus they seek out the most punishing of experiences: striving to eat no more or differently than starving nineteenth-century soldiers might, for instance, and to endure extremes of heat and cold, bugs and blisters, sleep deprivation and physical exhaustion. In this way, contemporary reenactors resemble the strenuous-life adherents of the previous century, sharing with them a longing to escape the stultifying or alienating confines of modern life through the cultivation of intense, embodied experience, pursued through largely homosocial activities staged in the out-of-doors.

As we see in chapter 2, this fantasy of intense embodied experience circulates persistently if paradoxically through cinematic simulations as well: the most popular and widespread form of battle reenactment. Indeed, live reenactments have many things in common with their cinematic brethren, including an intense investment in notions of authenticity that plays out in relation to both the material foundations of war-making and the suffering that war-making entails. Suffering provides an explicit focus for war films as for reenactors who "identify with the soldier not only as history's hero but also as history's long-suffering victim" (Apel 54). Whereas war reenactors highlight bodily suffering while bracketing the simulation of graphic casualties, however, war films invest heavily in the graphic image of bodily trauma as a signifier of the real.

The investment in suffering as a privileged source of authenticity is also suggested in the training of actors themselves, who frequently undergo pseudomilitary regimes to ready themselves not for combat but for its reenactment onscreen. Like the hidden stitches on the hobby reenactor's uniform, not all of this effort is readily visible, but it is imagined to inform authenticity at a deeper level. Actors can come to know and understand something of the experience of war through such war games and thus more successfully communicate this knowingness to an audience (or so the argument goes). In preparation for filming the Vietnam War film *Platoon* (dir. Stone, 1986), for instance, actors attended a two-week boot camp in the Philippine jungle, overseen by the decorated Vietnam veteran (and Hollywood consultant) Dale Dye. They were issued dog tags, M-16 rifles, ponchos, red-filtered flashlights, bayonets, canteens, and other gear. They lived on rations; dug foxholes, in which they slept in two-hour shifts; marched for miles with sixty-pound packs on their backs; and withstood simulated enemy ambushes and mortar attacks (Rubin; Goodgame). The experience was imagined to ready the actors to embody grunts on the ground: according to the actor Willem Dafoe, "the training was a kind of initiation that made us somehow worthy to tell the story" (Rubin 196).

Similar immersive exercises are undertaken by the designers of videogames, as in the example of Steven Spielberg's *Medal of Honor* (DreamWorks Interactive, 1999) team, required—like the cast of *Saving Private Ryan* (dir. Spielberg, 1998)—to undergo military-style boot camp. The civilian programmers, designers, and marketers of the Army's videogame *America's Army* likewise undergo simulated training. In working on the design of

America's Army: Special Forces (2003), for instance, the team traveled to a Special Forces training ground in Wyoming, where they practiced firing weapons, rode in Black Hawk helicopters, and drilled alongside the soldiers, in an effort to deepen the "feel" of war that gameplay delivers (Schiesel). Groups from the Army Game Project have also trained at the Army Training Center in Fort Jackson, where they undergo a "mini" basic training course in an effort to introduce into gameplay "an experiential taste of boot camp" (R. Allen 152): "what it sounds like, what it feels like, even what it smells like," according to *America's Army*'s originator, Colonel Casey Wardynski (Bourke 197). In both film and videogames, then, the striving toward realism emphasizes graphical fidelity while chasing after more ephemeral aspects of the real, such as the smells, sounds, heat, cold, creeping fear, and adrenaline rush of combat experience.

While these examples emphasize the military exercises of Hollywood actors and videogame designers, mobilizing "the magic of Hollywood" in support of military training itself is the express mission of Strategic Operations, Inc. (STOPS). Located at a large independent television and movie studio near San Diego, Strategic Operations plays host to the U.S. military as well as federal, state, and local policing agencies, supplying them with a broad range of "Hyper-Realistic" training scenarios. These scenarios are supported by an army of role-players—from insurgents to government officials to civilians to a full platoon of special operations forces (all supplied by an on-site casting agency)—alongside pyrotechnic and other special effects personnel. The impact of these simulations is augmented by Hollywood-style sets "complete with props and atmospherics" and an array of "Hyper-Realistic" casualties intended to amplify the simulation's "stress inoculation factor" (Strategic Operations). While Hollywood seeks to militarize its products through authentic training regimes, then, the military (here as at Fort Irwin) draws on entertainment studio sets, technicians, and technologies to bolster the efficacy of realism itself.

The examples of live wargaming discussed in this chapter work to manage and contain the messy, chaotic, unpredictable contingencies of real war, even as they seek to simulate a sense of bodily risk, deprivation, and strain. This paradox informs cinematic reenactments as well, which constitute violence as a voyeuristic spectacle while inviting an intensely visceral feeling of involvement in the scene of battle. As hinted at in the STOPS example, Hollywood provides a powerful guide to other forms of war simulation, as "simulation is always dependent on the player's *image* of the subject being simulated" (Nakamura 46): in this case, an image centrally informed by the history of war onscreen. To look or feel authentic has very often meant to look or feel like the movies. It is thus to screen-based simulations of war that we now turn.

2

ONSCREEN

Like the war games of chapter 1, simulations of war onscreen have served a variety of purposes across different and often overlapping contexts, including military training, combat, and therapy, as well as news and entertainment. More than any other mode of war play, they have shaped the cultural imagination of what "real" war looks and feels like. In this chapter and the next, we survey these screen-based simulations to consider their role in the imagination and the waging of war. This chapter focuses on film (and to a lesser extent television) in relation to questions of authenticity and realness in particular and traces the appeals of both grunt's-eye and god's-eye views as they resonate with the perspectives of live war games and reenactments. Chapter 3 shifts attention to interactive forms of screen-based war games, including training simulations and videogames.

The simulation of war onscreen revolves around a central tension between the conviction that war is beyond representation—unrepresentable in its essence—and the ongoing investment in representing it in realistic or authentic ways. In the face of this tension, a variety of conventions have emerged, many focused around generating intense visceral sensations in the bodies of film and television viewers: the feeling of "being there" amid the action and violence of combat. In these examples, the body of the spectator is positioned as the locus of realness itself, as realness registers and is evaluated as and at the level of feeling. This is conspicuously true of the landmark *Saving Private Ryan,* for instance, and much of the war media that follows, including films, embedded newscasts, first-person shooter games (FPS), and helmet-cam videos. But it is also true of films earlier in the twentieth century, including World War II combat reports and post-Vietnam feature films such as *Platoon* and others.

We can recognize the impulse to represent war through the aggressive appeals of "being there" even in the earliest moving pictures of the late 1890s and early 1900s, when imperialist ventures such as the Spanish-American and Philippine-American Wars provided profitable material for the nascent film industry. In the charge films and battle reenactments of these early years, the action and violence of war are presented in viscerally engaging terms, as infantry open fire directly toward the front of the frame and cavalry storm the camera position (and by extension the cinema audience). In *Charge of the Seventh French Cuirassiers* (dir. Lumière, 1896), shown at an early screening in New York City, the advance of the horses toward the camera was described in the press as both "realistic" and "thrilling." Catalog copy for the *Charge of Boer Cavalry* (dir. Edison, 1900) a few years later applauded the film's ability to elicit a physical response from its audience, who "[make] an involuntary effort to move from their seats in order to avoid being trampled under the horses" (Eagle 52). In these and other examples, the most compelling moving pictures of war were associated both with visceral thrills and with realism, highlighting the early link between sensationalism and realist entertainment.

The association of the real with the thrilling relates to cultural ideas about war itself as defined by intense embodied experiences of action and violence that stand in contrast to the often staid or enervating routines of daily life. The lived experience of war is usually dominated by other kinds of experience: waiting, boredom, immobility, and strenuous physical labors divorced from excitement or glory (the building of trenches, cleaning of equipment, marching with heavy packs in extremes of heat and cold, to name a few). The cultural imagination of "real" war as both exciting and glorious has persisted, however, fed in no small part by the popular construction of war onscreen. The lived experience of war is often narrated back through reference to these screen-based attractions, so that moments of intense action and violence are described as "like a movie" or, more recently, "like a videogame." This underscores a second, related tension animating representations of war: that realness has been produced not in opposition to simulation but very much through and in relation to it.

Realistic war representation has also relied on the status of the objects (and sometimes the people) appearing before the camera. The earliest war films make no clear distinction between documentary-style images and those staged explicitly for the camera: as a category of film production, these military "actualities" were understood to represent real events regardless of their provenance or the glaring inaccuracies of their settings or effects (a naval battle might be fought in a bathtub, for instance; and African American actors could portray rebel Filipinos, advancing with a marked lack of conviction through the New Jersey woods). By the World War I drama *The Unbeliever* (dir. Crosland, 1918), however, the participation of the Marine Corps provides the foundation for the film's claims to authenticity. In a similar vein, Pathe's *J'Accuse* (dir. Gance, 1919) features two thousand French troops on leave from the fighting at Verdun. Films made after the war continue this trend, as in *The Big Parade* (dir. Vidor, 1925) and the seminal *All Quiet on the Western Front* (dir. Milestone, 1930), which highlight the use of period uniforms and materiel as part of their commitment to realism.

By the second half of the century, the authenticity of weapons, uniforms, and equipment takes a central place in the cinematic reenactment of war (even as the early merger of staged with documentary footage continues and increasingly blurs in the context of digital cinema). As in the battle reenactments of chapter 1, for historical conflicts in particular, period detail is directly linked to the perceived value and credibility of war onscreen: in screen-based as in live environments, the simulation of war is understood to depend on these material foundations. This investment in authenticity is also evident in the much-touted involvement of past or present members of the military in a given production, as advisers, documentary "talking heads," or semifictionalized characters, as in the soon-to-be-deployed Marines in *The Unbeliever* or the active Navy SEALS in *Act of Valor* (dir. McCoy and Waugh, 2012) almost a century later. The appeal of war onscreen has relied on these notions of authenticity alongside and in combination with the melodramatic conventions of fiction filmmaking.

Another key element in the construction of realness onscreen is the indexicality of film as a photographic medium. As defined by the philosopher C. S. Peirce, an index designates a particular kind of sign, or a particular kind of relationship between a sign and the object it references. Peirce defined symbols as signs in which the relationship between the sign and its object is arbitrary, based on habit or convention rather than on a physical connection or resemblance. Signs based on relations of resemblance he designated as icons. Indexical signs, in contrast, bear an existential or causal relationship to their referent, as in the example of a weather vane indicating the presence of the wind, or a photograph, in which the image represents an imprint of light bouncing off an object. Like all indexical signs, the photograph (or the strip of celluloid composed of a series of photographs) attests to the existence of the object it references.

The indexical relationship between the onscreen image and the object it represents has contributed to ideas of truth in the genre of war documentaries in particular. In this context, the shared space and time of the camera and the object or action it films testify to the realness of the image onscreen and invite the viewer to share in the sense of presence that this image constructs. As we shall see, this sign of realness carries over into fictional war films as well, through formal techniques that highlight the camera's presence on the scene of action. And while digital cinema unsettles the indexical relationship between an onscreen image and the object it represents, it continues to reference the legacy of film as a photographic medium (even when the felt presence of the camera may be itself an algorithmic construction). The force of the photographic index persists in the context of the image's digitization, as in the example of Peter Jackson's *They Shall Not Grow Old* (2018), which brings cutting-edge technologies to bear on documentary images of World War I, adjusting the speed, sharpening and colorizing the historical footage—which is rendered now in 3-D—and adding in sound, including dubbed dialog decoded with the help of lip readers. If critical response is any guide, we are compelled by the truth of these images not less but more in the face of their digital manipulation, highlighting how contemporary cinematic conventions shape our apprehension of the real onscreen, as the film offers an "intensified vision of all the old feelings," paradoxically heightening our sense "that this really did happen to people like you and me" (Bradshaw).

AUTHENTIC VIOLENCE AND THE WORLD WAR II COMBAT REPORTS

The combat reports of World War II—military documentaries of two to four reels, released to home-front theaters for broad public screening—provide one powerful example of how the felt presence of the camera works to produce a sense of realness onscreen. Through these documentaries, a new realistic aesthetic takes shape, one that emphasizes the visceral sense of "being there" amid the action. Despite the fact that radio and print relayed information far more quickly, for audiences in the 1940s, combat reports and newsreels represented an unprecedented feeling of proximity to the news of war, while also providing narrative and stylistic frameworks to help order and contain this news and the sense of chaos it threatened.

Operating under the auspices of the Army Signal Corps, the Navy Photographic Unit, and the Marine Corps, military photographers produced an extraordinary visual record of the war, including footage for commercial newsreels and screen magazines, official military combat reports, training and propaganda (or "morale") films, and reconnaissance films. In the field and stateside at the Army's Photographic Center in New York, enlisted men worked alongside civilian newsreel crews and Hollywood directors, cinematographers, and other studio personnel recruited into military service (Koszarski). Trained in courses taught by newsreel companies and later by Hollywood personnel, military combat photographers learned to internalize the codes and conventions of commercial filmmaking, including framing, camera angle and distance, and screen direction, to "instinctively sho[ot] pictures that 'made sense' on the screen" (Doherty 251). By the outbreak of World War II, the established role of newsreels and the cultural dominance of the cinema meant that millions of people were consuming news of the war through these images: in the United States alone, eighty-five million people went to the movies weekly by 1939, close to three-quarters of the country's total population; and the most successful combat reports received theatrical billing equal to that of the latest Hollywood feature.

A photographic record of war had informed the American imagination since the Civil War, and moving pictures had also played a part in previous conflicts. Cameramen accompanied U.S. troops to Cuba in 1898 in the hopes of capturing moving images of battle, and while no live combat footage resulted, scenes of U.S. troops landing and other views from Cuba and the Philippines appeared alongside staged battles and charge films in war-themed programs across the country at the end of the nineteenth and beginning of the twentieth centuries. Moving pictures were also central to the much-documented Mexican Revolution, in which the revolutionary general Pancho Villa signed a contract with the Mutual Film Corporation to facilitate the filming of his military exploits.

During World War I, nonfiction films such as *War as It Really Is* (1916) and advertisements touting "all the thrills of genuine warfare" confirm the explicit appeal to realness that was well established in promotional discourse by this time (Abel). The feature-length military actuality *Battle of the Somme* (dir. Malins, 1916)—which showed "war as war is, in all its real reality" (Hammond, *Big* 126)—received a tremendous reception in commercial movie houses in England while the battle itself wore on in France. Meanwhile, the director D. W. Griffith, renowned for his massive staging of Civil War battles for *The Birth of a Nation* (1915), voiced his disappointment over the lack of epic spectacle on the Western Front, where he had traveled in the hopes of attaining exciting combat footage: an early instance of real war disappointing its cinematic anticipation.

It was not until World War II, however, that the relationship between war and film was fully established. The wartime combat reports and newsreels offered a novel kind of combat cinematography enabled by faster film stock and more portable lightweight cameras that allowed for filming in a greater range of environments, including especially the filming of live action. This was strikingly on view in the first official combat report released to home-front theaters, the director John Ford's *The Battle of Midway* (1942). The film—shot on color stock by Ford and the cameraman Jack MacKenzie Jr. during fighting on Midway Atoll—is composed of a striking combination of familiar sentimental conventions and raw combat footage. In the film's most famous shots, which repeat twice across the battle sequence, the image jerks and blurs abruptly as the film is jolted out of its frame by the impact of an exploding shell nearby: a vivid index of the violence. The inclusion of this shot in the film's final cut was much commented on at the time, as it broke starkly with the stable frame and clear focus of classical Hollywood filmmaking. This indexing of war violence became quickly conventionalized in the combat reports to follow, in which the jerking, blurring, and shaking of the image inscribe the rapid, irregular movements of camera operators and the concussive impacts of nearby explosions. Such techniques highlight what the film scholar Thomas Doherty has called a "verisimilitude-via-deficiency," as the violation of classical Hollywood conventions amplifies the sense of realness and the felt presence of the camera on the scene of violence (254).

In considering the kind of "realness" the combat reports construct, it is useful to recall how the training of the combat photographers encouraged their internalization of the rules and norms of Hollywood filmmaking. Shooting with these in mind, they edited in camera as much as possible, to produce footage that would lend itself readily to established formal and narrative structures. In addition, combat photographers knew that their footage would be heavily censored and often shot accordingly, avoiding the most gruesome scenes—especially those featuring U.S. and Allied casualties—in an effort to more efficiently marshal their limited supply of film stock. In some cases, their own sense of propriety determined the choice of where (and where not) to direct their cameras, adding a layer of self-censorship to the internalization of official norms. Thus, while the reports represent war with a new kind of rawness and immediacy, it is important to remember the conventions that shaped these official records of war, with regard to both what the camera recorded and what was excluded from the frame.

The war gave rise to newly fluid relationships between documentary and commercial filmmaking, with the influx of studio personnel into the military and the commercial studios' broad adoption of the realist aesthetics of the military documentaries. In addition to incorporating actuality footage into feature-length fiction films—a practice facilitated by the formation of the Academy of Motion Picture Arts and Sciences' War Film Library—Hollywood directors and cinematographers tried to reproduce in the studio the effects that had originally signified the presence of the camera (and its operator) in the midst of combat action. In Howard Hawks's *Air Force* (1943), for example, a shaky camera is used to suggest the bumpy ride of a B-17 bomber from the perspective of its turbulent interior. Here the jerking and blurring of the image that had represented a dramatic violation of convention in *The Battle of Midway* form part of a new filmmaking grammar. In developing this technique, the cinematographer James Wong Howe explicitly identified his intent as "giving the audience a sense of real participation" (Zimmerman 111).

At the same time, an audience raised on studio war films brought to the viewing of military documentaries a set of expectations for excitement and dramatic action, as well as coherence and larger meaning, that combat footage alone could not deliver. Though the combat reports were often imagined as a transparent window onto the raw truth of war, their "realness" relied on a combination of techniques and appeals, many of them bearing a Hollywood pedigree. The film critic James Agee came to praise as most authentic the hybrid "semifictional" films such as Hollywood's *The Story of G.I. Joe* (dir. Wellman, 1945), in which documentary and melodramatic forms combine (Youra 27). And even *The Battle of Midway* ordered and contained its chaotic combat images within a sentimental frame—relying on voice-overs, a dramatic score, and bookending its central combat sequence with a series of melodramatic tableaux—lest the sense of a larger meaning or moral slip like the film strip in Ford's camera. Indeed, it is the combination of familiar melodramatic techniques with the new and startling appeals of combat cinematography that made *The Battle of Midway* so affecting.

The shift toward a less studio-bound look in Hollywood films during and after the war spoke to the tastes and expectations of an audience acclimated to a new kind of realism through the combat reports and newsreels. Alongside the appeal to vicarious experience, however, there was also the question of cinematic spectacle and its distancing, voyeuristic implications. As Agee suggests, the degree to which the "war-record films" signified the realness and proximity of war was complicated by the degree to which they might induce numbness in their viewers, ultimately limiting rather than encouraging audience identification with those who fought. In the visceral address of the combat reports, Agee believed film had reached the pinnacle of its empathetic power as a medium uniquely suited to conveying the horror and brutality of war. By the end of the war, however, he had begun to reconsider. Rather than collapsing the distance between combatants and a stateside audience, he worried that the inherent remove of viewers from the violence onscreen constituted a kind of obscenity, as they watched the act of killing "hopelessly incapable of reactions adequate to the event" (152). The tension that Agee highlights is one that is still relevant today, as filmmakers, scholars, politicians, and the public continue to debate the ethical, psychological, and social implications of "realistic" violence onscreen.

SAVING PRIVATE RYAN AND THE REENACTMENT OF THE REAL

When Steven Spielberg was looking to up the realist ante in re-creating the landing of U.S. troops on the Normandy coast in *Saving Private Ryan,* he turned to combat reports such as *The Battle of Midway, With the Marines at Tarawa* (dir. Hayward, 1944), and *The Battle of San Pietro* (dir. Huston, 1945), alongside Robert Capa's still photographs of the landing (Haggith). Replicating the low angle of the combat photographer's camera, the film's famed Omaha Beach sequence pulls the viewer into an intense and harrowing sense of presence amid the carnage. The violence is elaborately staged to highlight a degree of graphic detail unprecedented in the war film genre as, enveloped in a chaotic scene of suffering, confusion, and death, we witness across the twenty-four-minute sequence the impact of bullets and explosives on bodies: the soldier who grasps at his guts as they spill out onto the sand; the soldier who dazedly turns to collect his own dismembered arm; the torrents of blood that stain the beach and ocean red.

The sequence employs a variety of techniques heralded for the intensity and immediacy they bring to the film's representation of violence. The use of a handheld camera fitted with the then-new Image Shaker lens re-creates the vibrations caused in the original combat reports by the impact of exploding shells. Images blur to suggest the chaotic movements of a camera operator on the ground (although in the case of Capa's pictures, the blurring was the result of a darkroom error rather than an index of Capa's own "agitation and movement under fire," as Spielberg had assumed; Haggith 335). The lens is splattered with blood and splashed with water as the camera jerks and weaves through the scene of massacre on the beach and bobs up and down among the sinking bodies of soldiers as blood flowers into the sea around them, highlighting the active presence of the camera amid the violence it depicts. To connote the look of the source material, Spielberg and his cinematographer, Janusz Kaminski, desaturate the color to suggest 1940s film stock, strip the camera lens of its modern protective coating, and adjust the shutter angle to produce a starker image and a more staccato quality of movement onscreen.

In the sound design too, the film strives for a realist aesthetic defined by the experience of war on the ground. Across the sequence, the soundtrack eschews any musical score. It cuts to a muted near silence after Captain Miller

(Tom Hanks) is momentarily deafened by an exploding mortar shell, inviting identification with the altered sensorium of war. At the level of exhibition, the film capitalized on the still-novel technology of digital surround sound, sonically immersing the audience in battle in unprecedented ways (Decker 130).

Critical and popular response offered a vigorous testament to the efficacy of the sequence in bringing the viewer into an overwhelming, visceral sense of presence with the violence onscreen. Though the film largely reverts to generic form after the Omaha Beach landing (and though many of the techniques used by Spielberg had in fact been explored in earlier reenactments), *Saving Private Ryan* is widely acknowledged as setting a new standard for realist war representation, one that would inspire subsequent films as well as other media such as videogames. "By far the biggest and most expensive attempt to represent battle in the entire history of the cinema," the film works to produce credibility through "sheer massed 'authenticity'" (Ascherson). In addition to the camera work and effects designed to suggest the "look" of 1940s combat photography, this authenticity is signified through the objects and actors placed before the camera: the vast accumulation of historical and re-created hardware; the meticulous attention to uniforms and weapons; the military training of the actors themselves and the use of veterans and active soldiers as extras (as in the reenactments at Fort Irwin, amputees are employed to portray the wounded). Though there are some postproduction effects, the sequence relies primarily on special effects on set, in an effort to heighten the authentic experience of combat for the actors and audience both.

As Spielberg has emphasized, a desire to "re-sensitize the audience" (Ressner) to the suffering endured by World War II veterans motivated many of his choices, a motivation that resonates with Agee's ideas about the combat reports as providing an ethically necessary and socially useful vicarious exposure to violence. This notion of resensitization, however, is a complex one. The Omaha Beach sequence, in its graphic representation of violence, resembles not the extant footage of Normandy so much as *With the Marines at Tarawa*. While footage of the Western Front did not tend to linger on images of the Axis dead, the same sensibility did not extend to war in the Pacific, and *Tarawa* is noteworthy for its visual emphasis on Japanese casualties. In restaging an authentic record of the war, then, *Saving Private Ryan* mobilizes images of bodily suffering that, in the context of the combat reports themselves, only appeared through the representation of these enemy bodies. In *Tarawa*, images of death and suffering are offered to the home-front audience as a source of sadistic satisfaction, in line with the racist rhetoric of contemporary war propaganda. In the Spielberg film, similar images invite identification with the position of U.S. troops as victims of a brutal assault (a construction that resonates with the melodramatic tradition of Hollywood cinema as it constitutes the virtuous through the image of their suffering; Eagle). The racist representational politics of the original reports are thus both referenced and erased in Spielberg's reenactment.

While *Saving Private Ryan* draws on the combat reports to authenticate its vision of real war, the reports themselves incorporated reenacted footage far more than was acknowledged at the time. Despite official orders to use actual battle scenes only, for instance, in *The Battle of San Pietro*—a film praised as a "masterpiece of experienced immediate horror" (Gold 20)—combat was reconstructed almost entirely for the camera. The British *Desert Victory* (dir. Boulting and MacDonald, 1943) was heralded as "the first serious attempt to make an audience participate in war" and commended for its eschewal of "tricks and frills," even as it relied on reenacted footage of battle on the North African Front (Agee 34). In *Attack! The Battle for New Britain* (1944), when the need for particular continuity shots arose during the editing process, camera crews returned to the site of filming to capture additional footage of the U.S. Marines, who directed the crews to choice sites and initiated combat on queue to comply with their requirements (Maslowski 71)—this despite the film's opening assurance that "the picture you are about to see is authentic in every detail. No scenes have been reenacted or staged."

A final example of *December 7th* (dir. Ford and Toland, 1943) helps to highlight how these reenactments resonate across the popular memory of war. Like *The Battle of Midway, December 7th* was an Academy Award winner for Documentary Short Subject. Due to the very limited amount of footage that had been shot during the attack on Oahu in 1941, the film relies on elaborately crafted sequences in which a modicum of extant footage is intercut with reenacted scenes of individual soldiers under fire (shot with a handheld camera to mimic the look of other combat reports), dramatic backlot battles featuring miniature ships and planes, and other special effects. While parts of the film are staged quite explicitly (especially in its originally unreleased long version), the film's battle sequences offered an influential source of documentary imagery both during and after the war. These reenacted sequences served as the model for director Michael Bay's 2001 film *Pearl Harbor* (White and Yi 330). A mix of historical and simulated imagery likewise informs *Attack: Battlefied Oahu* (Aperture Films, 2010), a short "immersive documentary" that plays on a loop at the Valor in the Pacific National Monument at Pearl Harbor. In this as in many others examples, the cinematic reenactment of war becomes an enduring source of official as well as popular memory—a point to which we will return.

In imitating and augmenting the reality of the combat reports, Spielberg crafts a highly aestheticized vision of the Normandy landing, one that starkly contrasts a contemporary description of the beaches as looking like a "poorly organised and fairly dull beach party" (Haggith 344). This augmentation makes sense in light of the director and Vietnam veteran Samuel Fuller's assertion that "you can't see anything in actual combat," so to represent it authentically, "you'd have to blind the audience with smoke, deafen them with noise, then shoot one of them in the shoulder to scare the rest to death" (Maslowski 73). Cinematic realism, then, may be less a matter of authenticity and more a matter of the visceral and emotional intensity with which a film addresses its audience. Understood this way, we can make sense of the critical evaluation of *San Pietro* as representing the reality of war more effectively than reality itself might or of the assertion that, in watching *Saving Private Ryan,* one viewer "felt ultimate reality several times" (Hammond, *Saving* 153). These comments speak to the ability of film to condense and amplify the felt significance of lived experience in a way that effectively captures something of the essence of that experience. Thus, the reenacted, staged, or stylized cannot be opposed to the realistic in any clear or simple way, as (in the words of the British director Anthony Asquith) "a non-realistic scene can be realler than the real thing" (27).

Two points follow from this: that the realness of war representation has to do with more than simply the indexical recording of a pro-filmic reality and that lived experience itself does not operate free from the influence of cinema's representation of it. The realism of war onscreen is produced through documentary signs and techniques in combination with the conventions and appeals of fiction filmmaking. In the documentaries of World War II, novel images of combat on the ground were framed and shaped by familiar Hollywood conventions. Rather than undercut a film's claim to realness, these stylistic and thematic elements served to heighten, or even to constitute, such a claim. Even in *Saving Private Ryan,* though some reviewers noted the authenticity of the landing sequence in contrast to the more conventional genre film that follows, the film's sense of realness depends on its familiar melodramatic framing. An appreciation of this intertwining of documentary with fictional appeals enables us to make sense of the paradoxical, if persistent, assertion that film—in all its artfulness—can offer us a vision "more real than the real thing" (Asquith 26). Rather than simply a reflection of reality, film actively works to constitute and define what we understand to be real, in war films perhaps more than in any other genre.

VIETNAM ON BIG SCREENS AND SMALL

As we see in the preceding examples, war films themselves serve as a privileged referent for war representation: to look authentic, *Saving Private Ryan* and *Pearl Harbor* must look like combat reports from the 1940s more than like war "itself." That World War II veterans affirmed the authenticity of *Saving Private Ryan*'s Omaha Beach sequence suggests the relationship of war experience to the mediated history of war. Even for those who fight, the movies have provided a reference point, shaping lived experience in complex and often contradictory ways and intermingling with its memory afterward.

The merger of lived with mediated experience is highlighted in accounts of soldiers who fought in the Vietnam War. For many of these men, the Hollywood films of World War II had shaped a set of expectations that were difficult to shake. World War II was the country's "good war," its moral purpose a point of broad national consensus. But mediated fantasies of good war played out quite differently in the "moral quagmire" of Vietnam, with its profound disruption of the narratives of national and martial virtue. In *Dispatches,* the acclaimed memoir of the war correspondent Michael Herr, the author describes the self-conscious (and self-annihilating) performances of soldiers in front of television crews, "actually making war movies in their heads, doing little guts-and-glory Leatherneck tap dances under fire, getting their pimples shot off for the networks" (209). These young men—media freaks, Herr calls them, though not unsympathetically—were "wiped out by seventeen years of war movies before coming to Vietnam to be wiped out for good." "We'd all seen too many movies," Herr opines, "stayed too long in Television City. . . . It was the same familiar violence, only moved over to another medium" (209). Echoing Herr's account, one veteran remarked, "It took me six months in Vietnam to wake up and turn all the World War II movies off in my mind" (Sturken 95). A decade later, when the veteran William Adams was asked about the accuracy of the film *Platoon*, he asserted that "no matter how graphic and realistic, a movie is after all a movie, and war is only like itself." But in the same breath, he suggested the hybrid nature of memory: "what 'really' happened is now so thoroughly mixed up in my mind with what has been said about what happened that the pure experience is no longer there" (Sturken 86).

Released alongside the cycle of revisionist Vietnam fantasies of which *Rambo: First Blood Part II* (dir. Cosmatos, 1985) was the most spectacular example, films such as

Platoon, Full Metal Jacket (dir. Kubrick, 1987), *Hamburger Hill* (dir. Irvin, 1987), and *Casualties of War* (dir. DePalma, 1989) emphasized realism and authenticity as a central part of their appeal. These films focused on a "grunt's-eye view" of Vietnam on the ground. The mud-splashed camera lens in *Platoon*'s opening sequence recalls the indexical signs of presence that distinguished the World War II combat reports (and anticipates Spielberg's appropriation of these signs in *Saving Private Ryan*). That *Platoon* was written and directed by Oliver Stone, himself a Vietnam veteran, was heavily promoted to help authenticate its vision. Promotional materials and critical reception both asserted the close proximity of the film's reenactment to the lived experience of the war: "Viet Nam as It Really Was," declared *Time* magazine's cover on January 26, 1987. As David Halberstam presciently suggested in 1987, "thirty years from now, people will think of the Viet Nam War as *Platoon*" (Sturken 97).

The investment of this cycle of films in a grunt's-eye view helped to shift the war film as a genre toward more viscerally intense and sensually engaging representations. A description of documentaries produced during the war captures an impulse shared by these later fiction films as, in "re-creat[ing] a trip to the front," films such as *Platoon* worked to produce the movie theater as a theater of war, in which an audience might be "made to experience phenomenally the textures and terrors of battle" (James 242; a formulation that highlights the kinship between film and other modes of war play such as live battle reenactments). In *Platoon,* the wet, thick heat of the jungle, abundant with threatening life—snakes, ants, leeches, and snipers—is made palpable through a camera that clings claustrophobically close to the soldiers. The film emphasizes the fatigue and boredom of the war, alongside its terror and chaos. In the close alignment of the camera with the perspective of the grunts, there is often little way for the audience to orient itself within any larger ordering framework—a thematic that underscores the lack of narrative coherence or moral direction signified by the war itself.

With an explicit emphasis on how war feels, films such as *Platoon* produce individual experience as the locus of understanding. As noted in chapter 1 (and like the cast of *Saving Private Ryan* a decade later), as part of Stone's effort to collapse the distance between the film and the real historical experience it represented, the actors in *Platoon* were required to undertake a reenactment of their own prior to shooting: a punishing boot camp in the heat of the Philippine jungle intended to replicate the strains and deprivations of combat. For the actors as well as the audience, to know and come to terms with Vietnam, *Platoon* suggests, one must feel what the ground soldiers felt. In working to translate the experience of war into the language of cinema, the film positions watching a war film as akin to "a kind of veteranness" (Sturken 96). Having endured the agitations and discomforts of the war onscreen, viewers (in a manner not dissimilar to the war reenactors of chapter 1) might claim a certain kind of insight or at least the right to reflect on the national trauma of the war.

As World War II films shaped the imagination of soldiers in Vietnam, so did Vietnam War films shape the imagination of recruits to twenty-first-century wars in Afghanistan and Iraq. The Gulf War veteran Anthony Swofford notes the impact of Kubrick's *Full Metal Jacket* on his own decision to enlist. Watching the film, young men such as Swofford longed for the transformative brutality it portrayed, understanding it (whatever the film's own impulse toward critique) as "beautiful and profane and dangerous." Swofford's own memoir provided the basis for the Gulf War film *Jarhead* (dir. Mendes, 2005), which highlights the futility and frustrations of lived as compared to fantasized war experience, perpetuating a seemingly endless cycle.

While film has been central to the collective memory of the Vietnam War, however, the war is often referred to as the first television war (despite the presence of television cameras in Korea, when the medium was in its infancy). Television nightly news had taken over the function of the cinematic newsreels in the 1950s. The broadcasts expanded from fifteen to thirty minutes in 1963, alongside the escalating involvement of the United States in Vietnam. The appearance of war on television helped to shape the medium of television news, granting it authority as a serious form of reportage. In contrast to the weeks or even months that it took combat reports to reach the cinema screen, on television war footage from Vietnam could reach U.S. audiences in a matter of days, heightening the sense of immediacy. The style of the footage itself—rough and unproduced, emphasizing an embedded perspective—lent credibility to the images onscreen.

Vietnam is also called the living-room war, in reference to the central role of television both in the war and in U.S. domestic life by 1960. The phrase highlights the sense of proximity and intimacy that television news represented, as the evening broadcasts carried increasingly graphic and chaotic images of the war into the heart of family and domestic space. There is debate over the specific impact of these images on public opinion: whether they drove or merely reconfirmed shifting beliefs about the futility or morality of the conflict and whether the nightly appearance of a miniaturized war in homes across the country sensitized the public or rendered the spectacle of war banal, normalizing or even trivializing it in the process. Suggestive of the latter view, bombing missions themselves were described by pilots in the documentary *Hearts and Minds* (dir. Davis, 1974) as feeling like a game, meditated through "something like a TV screen." Despite these debates, however, there is no question that the coverage worked to shape the cultural imagination of war, both at the time and since.

The number of reporters and photographers in the field in Vietnam and the relative lack of restrictions on their movements generated footage very unlike that of the World War II newsreels and combat reports. Despite the effort to provide some coherence through editing and voice-overs, the television broadcasts provide a stark contrast to the highly produced reports of World War II. Rather than wider context or analysis, the broadcasts emphasize the look and feel of the war, including documentary footage of base operations as well as combat action. While prior to the Tet Offensive in January 1968, the tone of television news was fairly positive—resonating with the official line that all was going smoothly—even early on, there is often a sense of disorganization and a lack of structure to the footage itself. Even before Tet, the broadcasts could also be critical: in 1965, for instance, in CBS coverage of U.S. Marines torching the villages of Cam Ne with Zippo lighters and flamethrowers, amid the plaintive wails and protests of women, children, and the elderly, the onscreen reporter Morley Safer is visibly disturbed and openly incredulous.

During network broadcasts of the Tet Offensive three years later, the images of fighting in the streets of Saigon overwhelmed any attempt to provide an overarching narrative or clear understanding of what was unfolding onscreen. Even military officials interviewed on camera seemed confused and disoriented, unconvincing in their attempts to narrate the violence surrounding them. This was a significant moment in the shifting tides of public opinion, as the images on the news stood in stark contrast to official accounts of the war as noble, winnable, and progressing successfully. In the months after Tet, televised images of both civilian and military casualties increased significantly, and the tone of broadcasts shifted as well, encapsulated by the venerated anchorman Walter Cronkite's on-air characterization of the war as a "bloody stalemate."

The grunt aesthetic of *Platoon* and other films in this cycle owes much to this television reportage. In "'capturing the reality' of Vietnam on film, as if it were always escaping" (Berg 50), filmmakers mined the newscasts for an instantly recognizable iconography and a documentary look on the ground, with all the sense of authenticity that this look connoted. This lineage is made explicit in the mockumentary *84 Charlie MoPic* (dir. Duncan, 1989), presented from the first-person camera of an in-story documentarian. As in the case of *Saving Private Ryan* and the World War II combat reports, in appropriating the look of the television news, the Vietnam War films of the 1980s do not question the assumptions or priorities that shaped these newscasts to begin with—the lack of Vietnamese perspectives or engagement with the war's geopolitical conditions, for instance—as "fidelity to certain pictures and certain ways of picturing" continues to underwrite the popular memory of Vietnam (Berg 50).

The popular memory of subsequent wars would be shaped by very different modes of mediation. There was a dominant belief after Vietnam that televisual war reporting was anathema to popular endorsement of war: Nixon, for one, blamed the "relentless and literal reporting" of the war on television for the withdrawal of public support (Hallin 1). In subsequent conflicts, if there was to be any press access granted, this access would be a tightly restricted and closely managed affair. The British government, with the precedent of Vietnam in mind, restricted press access to fighting in the Falkland Islands in 1982, and the United States followed suit during its invasion of Grenada in 1983, during which journalists were banned and footage for newscasts was supplied instead by military camera crews.

In the face of both public and press outcry over these restrictions, a new system of press pooling was inaugurated, in which a limited number of selected journalists could gain access to troops and locations under close military escort. Though the pooling system offered little access during the invasion of Panama in 1989, by the Gulf War of 1991, the increasing integration of the press into the apparatus of the military shaped a new aesthetic of war on television, one profoundly divorced from the ground view of its predecessor. This aesthetic was conditioned also by the rapid corporate consolidation of the press across the 1980s and the drastic reduction in both the number of media outlets and the number of both investigative reporters and international news bureaus within them. In this context, news was centralized and largely homogenized, ripe for management through a tightly coordinated relationship between the press and the Pentagon and relying significantly on widely distributed video news releases produced by public-relations firms in the employ of the government itself (Andersen 172).

Coverage of the Gulf War was overwhelmingly focused on the spectacle of high-tech weaponry endowed with an almost magical degree of precision. Newscasts were structured like major sporting events, with themed graphics and music, highlights, replays, and color commentary. The war kicked off with a fiery display of the bombing of Baghdad live on television, carefully scheduled for prime-time viewing. In a newly invigorated twenty-four-hour news cycle, televisual discourse helped to construct the fantasy of a clean and surgical war of "smart" bombs and "precision-guided" missiles, a discourse founded on the erasure of missed targets and traditional dumb bombs that constituted the overwhelming majority of munitions.

The discourse of clean war pivoted on the profound dematerialization of violence. The bodies of Iraqi soldiers and civilians vanished completely through both the rhetoric of precision and the censorship of images of devastation on the ground. In addition, images of U.S. casualties—or the flag-draped coffins that signified their presence—were strictly prohibited, such that the war onscreen appeared free of any human cost. Televisual coverage focused instead on military hardware, detailed through labeled graphics and demonstrations that highlighted the capacities of new weapons technologies, underscoring the narrative of U.S. technological superiority. The soft targets of these technologies disappeared into collateral damage.

With the disappearance of the body went the signs of "real" war that had conventionally relied on it both as a visual focus and as a locus of perspective on the ground. Rather than situated in the midst of combat action, journalists were largely immobilized, bunkered in their hotel rooms as they reported on what they could see (or not see) and hear out their windows. Onscreen, they appeared as small headshots hovering over large maps. In place of their embodied perspective, television offered the perspective of the weapons themselves, through bomb's-eye-view footage captured from the nose of munitions as they fell. The blurry black-and-white image of a distant target in the crosshairs, growing quickly larger before disappearing into a field of static, was unlike anything that had appeared on television before. If Vietnam was the first television war, the Gulf War was called the first videogame war, framing the unfamiliar images through an emphasis on their game-like simulation, both highlighting and containing the ethical questions they posed. Appearing alongside the graphics of weapons and maps and the endless talking heads, the bomb's-eye views offered a sense of both immediacy and profound distance. In relation to the traditional you-are-there appeals of combat reporting on the ground, it was not at all clear where "there" really was.

SOMATIC WAR IN THE TWENTY-FIRST CENTURY

Very few movies were made about the Gulf War, though David O. Russell's *Three Kings* (1999) is noteworthy for its attempt to refuse the war's sanitized image by reintroducing the body onto the scene of violence, highlighting the sticky, visceral mess of war in the flow of blood, oil, excrement, and milk. Although *Three Kings* is stylistically distinct from *Saving Private Ryan,* both films emphasize the return to embodiment that would shape the aesthetic of war across media platforms by the opening of the twenty-first century. In Hollywood war films and the first-person shooter games they increasingly resembled, military-themed reality television and the embedded reporting it inspired, war onscreen would revolve around a first-person perspective in newly insistent and aggressive ways. Through a graphic emphasis on bodily violence and a visceral invitation into the simulated experience of combat, the body would come into focus again as a point of both representation and address, aligning war on film and television with other modes of war play.

The continued integration of the press into the apparatus of the military would both reflect and help to construct this embodied point of view. While during the Gulf War, media access was strictly curtailed, the practice of embedded reporting during the war's sequel in 2003 testified to a new level of coordination between the media and the Pentagon. Rather than the press being pooled and its movements restricted, journalists were assigned to the company and protection of specific military units, with which they traveled for the duration of the conflict. Embedding journalists as "member[s] of the team" was part of the government's self-described "product-marketing campaign" (Andersen 229): an effort to enlist the media in order to "sell" the war to the U.S. public. Donning helmets and exploring tanks, journalists functioned as surrogate war tourists for the audience back home, producing war as a thrilling adventure. Images of casualties and others considered to be in "poor taste" continued to be censored.

The embedding system, coupled with tight restrictions on content, encouraged a close focus on soldiers' experiences on the ground, laced with human-interest stories. The resemblance of this coverage to reality television was fairly earned, as the embedding system itself was inspired by the ABC-Pentagon coproduction *Profiles from the Front Line* (Warner Bros., 2003). The show—one of a host of Pentagon-supported reality shows of the early 2000s—was the brainchild of the public-relations expert Victoria Clarke (a key player in the most notorious faked accounts of the 1991 Gulf War; Stahl, *Militainment* 83–84). The first-person, ground-level perspective of embedded reporting also aligned it with the popular genre of the first-person shooter (to which we return in chapter 3).

Television was not alone in this symbiotic relationship, as Hollywood too worked closely with the Pentagon on a series of high-profile productions, which granted films access to hardware and personnel in exchange for military approval of scripts and other aspects of production. *Act of Valor,* a Navy recruitment ad developed into a feature-length film and (as noted) featuring active Navy SEALS in its starring roles, is one of the most conspicuous examples. As Tim Lenoir and Luke Caldwell observe, the film is structured like a videogame, with brief mission directives prefacing high-octane action outside of any political, social, or historical framework (190). Like most somatic war films, the form is episodic rather than linear. Other examples of the many films trading access for input include *Behind Enemy Lines* (dir. Moore, 2001), *Black Hawk Down* (dir. Scott, 2001), and *Zero Dark Thirty* (dir. Bigelow, 2012), discussed shortly. While the incorporation of genuine military hardware and personnel amplifies a film's claims to authenticity, according to one military spokesman, "any film that portrays the military as negative is not realistic to us" and is denied access to military resources on this basis (Bourke 183). Thus, the signs of realness accrue around both material and ideological aspects of filmmaking, as the authentication of military hardware is available only to films whose message aligns with official military goals, values, and perspectives: a critical view of the military is held to be inherently inauthentic.

The first-person perspective that defines somatic war films derives from overlapping histories of videogames, military simulations, and extreme sports that invite the spectator into an intensely visceral identification with movement, violence, and the vulnerability of the body at risk (McSorley). One central element constructing this perspective is helmet-mounted camera footage, which circulates through television newscasts, feature films and documentaries, and online video-sharing sites. With its insistent inscription of the visceral and kinesthetic experience of soldiering, the view from the "helmet-cam" is an emblem of somatic war: its shaky rhythms, quick pivots of attention, and sudden, disorienting bursts of action signify "the real" in a manner similar to the shakes and wobbles of the combat photographer's camera in World War II. The jittery camerawork and disjunctive cuts of the Best Picture winner *The Hurt Locker* (dir. Bigelow, 2008) attest to the influence of these emblematic rhythms on the contemporary visualization of war.

The night-vision footage of the "rescue" of Jessica Lynch, shot from a helmet-cam during the Iraq War in 2003 and circulated on television, highlights how this perspective aligns the viewer with both action and vulnerability. In this, helmet-cam footage resembles a first-person shooter, a correspondence that *Act of Valor* makes explicit in designing a helmet-cam expressly to mimic the "gamer POV" of an FPS (Lenoir and Caldwell 191). This conjunction, whereby to simulate a realistic soldiering experience we mimic the look and feel of a videogame, suggests the shared construction of militarized vision across military and recreational contexts. The intelligibility of this embodied vision, however, relies on other frameworks. As in both the Lynch rescue and *Act of Valor*, helmet-cam footage is generally contextualized within familiar narrative structures, edited into more traditional sequences, and accompanied by voice-over or soundtrack, in an effort to secure its meaning.

This is not to suggest that the weapon's-eye view, or the aerial view more generally, disappears in the context of somatic war. With the saturation of satellite vision in military as well as civilian contexts and the rapid ascendance of drone warfare in the twenty-first century, the view from above is newly ubiquitous. As the seminal thinker Paul Virilio has argued, the functions of the weapon and the eye have long coalesced, a conjunction most evident in the ascent of vision in war, first by watchtower, pigeon, and observation balloon, later by plane, satellite, and drone. To see is to target in these contexts, and as the ability to survey life on the ground in ever greater detail from ever greater points of remove increases, the omniscience and omnipotence imagined through the aerial view come sharply into focus. These appeals are made particularly explicit in the fantasy of unfettered access and mobility that drone technology conditions: a roving eye that can see and know all, and in the case of the military drone, not just an eye but a killer stare, equipped with the capacity to destroy.

The moral status of aerial vision is itself unsteady, however, as the voyeurism it connotes can align with sadism as well as divine provenance. We see an early example of this in the World War II report *Memphis Belle* (dir. Wyler, 1944), a documentary account of the final bombing run of the titular B-17 "Flying Fortress." The film mobilizes a variety of techniques—including voice-over, the individualization of the bombing crew, and an emphasis on the crew's own embodied vulnerability—to contain the morally unfixed implications of aerial vision at a time when air attacks were associated primarily with the barbarism of the enemy. By the turn of the twenty-first century, however, in an age of Google Earth and recreational drones, the integration of aerial vision into everyday life helps to cleanse it of these connotations. Though the sadism of the aerial view erupts into public discourse on occasion, underscoring Virilio's argument about the relationship between seeing and destroying, the aerial perspective has come to signify the global reach of a technologically enhanced and morally endowed imperial vision. Drone and satellite views enter the cinema in films such as *Black Hawk Down, Zero Dark Thirty,* and *Eye in the Sky* (dir. Hood, 2015). As films such as *Good Kill* (dir. Niccol, 2014) demonstrate, if there is a victim of drone vision in this context, it is often represented as the pilot himself.

The alternation between an embodied perspective on the ground and a disembodied one in the air is a central convention of war films in the twenty-first century. Even a World War II film such as *Hacksaw Ridge* (dir. Gibson, 2016), which cannot thematize drone or satellite technology directly, is drawn toward overhead shots, offering a more distanced, vaguely divine view from above as a brief respite from the gruesome scene of war that it is otherwise at pains to highlight. *Fury* (dir. Ayer, 2014), too, though its perspective remains resolutely on the ground, closes with an overhead shot of its titular tank surrounded by Nazi dead, securing an image of heroic sacrifice as the soundtrack swells.

We see the tension between ground and air first sketched out in *Black Hawk Down,* a film that heralds many of the impulses of somatic war. The film, whose release was pushed forward in the months after 9/11, offers a deeply revisionist account of failed U.S. military operations in Somalia in 1993, crafting a story of soldierly fealty among special operations forces and the heroic commitment to "leave no man behind." Early sequences replay familiar generic functions of aerial vision, mobilizing it in establishing shots and offering elegant views both of and from the Black Hawks as they soar over a beautiful beachfront (in a winking reference to *Apocalypse Now*; dir. Coppola, 1979). As the film progresses, however, the god's-eye view is revealed as largely impotent: real war resides emphatically below. While General Garrison (Sam Shepherd) fidgets and fumes before the grainy black-and-white satellite monitors, the film embeds the spectator amid the visceral assaults and sufferings of the soldiers on the ground.

In producing an immersive cinematic combat experience, the film looks and feels in many ways like a videogame. The focus on special operations forces resonates with contemporary military shooters, as does the conspicuous lack of character development among the men (who remain associated primarily with the actors who play them). This aligns with the conventional emphasis of gameplay on action rather than psychological interiority, with in-game characters granted a minimum of distinguishing features along the lines of the war film's "band of brothers." It is sensation rather than narrative or character that is primary in both contexts: a visceral identification with movement through space, with the violence that punctuates or impedes this movement, and with the state of embodied vulnerability that it conditions. In *Black Hawk Down*, the camera gravitates toward low-angle shots from the position of the soldiers as they crouch and scramble in the streets; some shots mirror directly the perspective of an FPS, featuring a weapon-wielding hand in the bottom foreground of the frame. As in the FPS, the film's emphasis on tactics over any broader geopolitical context lends itself to a racist depersonalization of the enemy Somali hordes, who swarm the screen like locusts (or like videogame zombies).

Critics reviewed the film as both the "most realistic" and the "most extravagantly aestheticized combat movie ever made" (Andersen 212), underscoring the enduring relationship between realism and sensationalism. Embraced simultaneously as highly realistic and heavily stylized, the film serves as a potent example of the "hyperbolic realism" that the film critic A. O. Scott later ascribed to *The Hurt Locker*. The "realness" of *Black Hawk Down* resides both in the frenetic pace of its rapid-cut, street-level action and in its graphic visualization of bodies ripped apart and torn to pieces, testaments to the centrality of an aggressive, visceral address in conceptions of real war onscreen.

The cinematic spectacle of real war is often constituted through cutting-edge effects and the new technologies that these display. In videogames too, technological advancements register as such to the extent that they are perceived to heighten fidelity to the real. In both media, then, what is hailed as most realistic operates at the same time as a marvel of simulation. The cinematic impulse to represent the real through both indexical signs and technological marvels can lead to a suggestive incoherence, as in the "over-the-shoulder" point-of-view shot (Crogan 68) from the perspective of a falling bomb in Bay's *Pearl Harbor* (a film that strives for "utmost realism," according to its director; Crogan 73). In this example, the digital image is painstakingly rendered to connote the wobbliness of a mythic camera operator (Allison 144), whose presence is belied by the technical virtuosity of the shot itself, which features the bomb as it plummets thousands of feet to bury itself in the USS *Arizona*. The shot suggests the desire to capture something ineffable about the force and impact of violence: here, to see and feel the "real" of war through the embodied perspective of a dropping bomb. Though this image harks back to the Gulf War's smart-bomb footage, while that image paradoxically signified the unmediated authenticity of violence, here the image attests instead to the technological magic of digital cinema.

The effort to capture the real of war through the signs of its violence is differently evinced in *Hacksaw Ridge*, a film that returns exhaustively, even compulsively, to the gruesome spectacle of the human body rendered as meat. If *Black Hawk Down* suggests that real war can be apprehended through the spectacular display of its bodily impact, *Hacksaw Ridge* takes this logic to its generic breaking point, teetering on the edge of a horror film. The film introduces its viewer to this horror through its protagonist, the conscientious objector Desmond Doss (Andrew Garfield), as he advances with his comrades over a field of bodies in all stages of death and putrefaction: the piles of guts squishing underfoot; the cadaver that springs to life only to be blasted apart; the severed heads; the mangled torso wielded as a shield; the rats as they feast on the corpses. The sequence returns repeatedly to these images as to a hellish talisman, as if by sheer accumulation, the graphic representation of the body rendered gruesomely thing-like might bring us closer to the real of war. Though *Hacksaw Ridge* is distinct from *Black Hawk Down* in look and tone, in both films this investment in graphic violence as an incontrovertible sign of the real appears in the context of an explicitly stylized—and in *Hacksaw Ridge,* a heavily sentimentalized—frame.

In focusing on the vulnerability of U.S. soldiers, *Hacksaw Ridge* carries on in the rescue tradition of films such as *Saving Private Ryan* (whose very title announces this project), *Behind Enemy Lines,* and *Black Hawk Down,* in which military purpose is defined not through or in relation to any geopolitical context but rather by the military's imperative "to continually save itself" (Stahl, *Crosshairs* 115). The emphasis on U.S. operatives as the locus of vulnerability and suffering—a dominant convention of twenty-first-century war films—includes *The Hurt Locker* and *Zero Dark Thirty,* which figure this suffering in psychological as well as physical terms. Both films feature the tortured or destroyed bodies of Middle Eastern others. Even in sequences that detail this violence, however, it is to the suffering of the American protagonists that our attention is inevitably directed. In the harrowing torture sequences of *Zero Dark Thirty,* for instance, it is with the discomfort of the CIA agent Maya (Jessica Chastain) in her position as a witness that the audience is invited most strongly to identify. And in *The Hurt Locker,* when the bomb specialist Will James (Jeremy Renner) defuses the body bomb he believes he recognizes as a local boy, it is on his psychological pain that we focus.

James's Kevlar bomb suit captures something of the paradox of U.S. power in its double play of vulnerability and invulnerability. The tank in *Fury* functions similarly, as a weapon of war that can turn with a flash into a furnace of death. In both cases, protagonists are rendered vulnerable by what makes them strong. In *Fury,* the paradox is intensified, as the tank crew is vastly outnumbered and rendered doubly vulnerable by their inferior machine, maintaining the conventional melodramatic position of the underdog despite the context of imminent Allied victory.

In *American Sniper* (dir. Eastwood, 2014) too, it is with the vulnerability of the protagonist, Chris Kyle, and his SEAL comrades that the film aligns our vision, even (or perhaps especially) as that vision is associated with Chris himself as "the most lethal sniper in U.S. history," as the film's promotional materials prominently state. This dynamic is twice encapsulated in the staging of standoffs between the sniper on the rooftop and his unwitting target below. In an entreaty that echoes across contemporary war films, Chris will threaten and plead—"Don't you do it!"—as he pulls back the trigger. Unaware down in the street, a child will pick up a weapon or he will not, and Chris will release his finger accordingly. Either way, we understand, it is the target that necessitates this violence and the shooter himself who is victimized by it. In highlighting the vulnerability of the man with the gun, *American Sniper* participates in the longer history of American melodrama, functioning as a metonym for the United States as a country that has long viewed even its most aggressive military actions as essentially defensive in nature (Eagle). The film's promotional poster nicely distills this dynamic, offering an elegiac black-and-white image of the hero as a portrait of pained vulnerability: star Bradley Cooper, his brow furrowed, his gaze downturned, psychically burdened by the very weapons that render him deadly.

The lethal gaze of the sniper, with all its attendant vulnerabilities, flows into the machinic vision of the drone, which surveys and destroys without direct risk to its operator (Stahl, *Crosshairs* 110). This double emphasis on the ever vulnerable body on the ground and the ascendant vision of an imperial eye in the sky makes for a powerful conjunction, if not always a stable one. As contemporary war films shuttle between the gun scope and the drone's stare, they merge different registers of what Roger Stahl has called the weaponized gaze (*Crosshairs*). Like the hybrid perspectives of videogames that shift between immersive first-person and commanding third-person views, this gaze shares in both the visceral excitements of war on the ground and the more ordered fantasies of command and control, recalling impulses of the live war games discussed in chapter 1. Despite the increasing normalization of the aerial view, however, the ethical issues entailed by this perspective—in which the subject of the gaze is granted both sight and agency over an objectified, unknowing, and unseeing other—require an ever more emphatic insistence on the vulnerability of U.S. troops on the ground. In keeping with the long-standing traditions of melodrama, as vulnerable the American soldier is rendered as virtuous and worthy of rescue.

The complex appeals of war films in the twenty-first century would make the genre itself a "toxic" one by many accounts: associated with box-office struggles and mixed reviews despite the conspicuous commercial success of *Black Hawk Down,* the unprecedented Oscar win of *The Hurt Locker* (the first for a female director), or the popular phenomenon of *American Sniper* (the highest grossing war film of all time). Nonetheless, the influence of cinematic simulations of war would continue to be felt, both within the contemporary imagination of war and within the exploding market of videogames, which would overtake the Hollywood box office to become "the most popular fictional depictions of America's current wars" (Suellentrop). It is to the appeals of interactive war games, then, that we turn next.

3
INTERACTIVE

Modes of simulation responsive to user input increasingly shape our relationship to war onscreen in both recreational and military contexts. We might think of these interactive simulations as battle reenactments that combine structures and impulses of the live gaming traditions of chapter 1 with the screen-based conventions of chapter 2. Despite significant distinctions between them, in these different modes of war gaming we can identify meaningful areas of overlap, shared histories, and common preoccupations.

In videogames, for instance, we recognize genres that emerged in the context of tabletop gaming, as well as a commitment to real-world fidelity, especially in regard to weapons and ballistics. Particular historical conflicts animate videogames, tabletop games, and live recreational reenactments, which share an overwhelming investment in the idea of authenticity. Like live reenactments, military shooters tend to eschew larger questions of social, political, or economic context. Gamers across these platforms traffic instead in highly detailed knowledge of military hardware and tactics.

In addition to a shared lineage with live war games, interactive war games bear an enormous debt to the screen-based traditions of chapter 2. They are shaped in many ways through the stylistic and generic conventions of the cinema even as they dramatically impact the look and feel of film itself. As we saw in chapter 2, the genre of the FPS in particular has contributed significantly to the aesthetic of somatic war; nonetheless, cinema has persisted as the "gold standard" by which the "realness" of videogame combat is often judged (Bourke 199). As in the cinema, the realism of interactive war games is defined through a mode of address explicitly oriented toward the agitation and excitation of the body, in combination with conventional elements of storytelling. The platforms through which users consume both films and videogames are largely overlapping in an age of digital convergence, transmedia franchises, mobile technologies, and 24/7 access to media flows. In this context, the conventions of cinema and videogames bleed into each other, influencing each other's aesthetics and thematics and trading characters and storyworlds back and forth between them.

Alongside the influence of cinema aesthetics, videogames frequently incorporate modes of authentication familiar from television news, including onscreen "reporters," documentary clips, and eyewitness accounts. At the same time, as the media scholar Roger Stahl has emphasized, after 9/11, television news begins to employ digital animations that are highly reminiscent of videogames (*Militainment* 92). In one striking example of the interplay between television and videogames, the World War II FPS *Brothers in Arms: Road to Hill 30* (Gearbox, 2005; which takes its title from the popular HBO miniseries *Band of Brothers* [2001]) inspired a History Channel documentary, *Brothers in Arms: The Untold Story of the 502* (2005). The television documentary then used gameplay sequences from the videogame in its own representation of the historical battle of the 502nd Parachute Infantry Regiment in Normandy (Lukas 85).

Videogames call on older forms of screen-based entertainment while constituting new modes of engagement with the simulated experience of war. The gamer seated before the console both resembles the cinema spectator and does not, just as gameplay both extends and alters familiar cinematic pleasures. Most significantly, the gamer engages not just with a screen but with a controller, enjoying a greater degree of agency—or at least a greater sense of agency—than the cinema spectator. Interactive media directly involve the actions of their users in the unfolding of a virtual world and, in networked multiplayer games, in real-time interactions with others, through a complex interplay of both subtle and overt responses to visual, auditory, tactile, and other stimuli. The interactivity of the medium extends to player-designed game modifications (or "mods") and the formation of online gaming communities.

While many of the threads traced through the previous chapters are relevant to this one, interactive media also raise new questions about the relationship between war gaming and war waging. Through the popularity of videogames, generations of young people have grown up fully acculturated to the mechanics, interfaces, and experiences of simulated combat. In the digital era, the waging of war can look and in some ways feel like its simulation. In the context of training simulations, the distinction itself may collapse (as the manufacturer of one such simulation boasts, for example, "trainees cannot distinguish between simulated signal displays and genuine signals"; T. Allen 285). As we have seen, as early as the Gulf War in 1991, the televisual bomb's-eye view reminded the public of nothing so much as a videogame. By the twenty-first century, the interactive systems, screen-based interfaces, and manual controllers of videogames come increasingly to resemble those of combat itself.

In the context of unmanned aerial systems in particular (also called unmanned aerial vehicles or, more commonly, drones), "real" and simulated interfaces can be identical. Both land and aerial remote-controlled weapons have been designed based on game consoles such as the PlayStation and the Xbox, in an effort to capitalize on soldiers' familiarity with these controls. Through these systems—in which the embodied experience of combat is mediated by screens, networked communications, and complex feedback loops—we witness a merger between war's gaming and its waging, as "the means of conducting real combat has also bent toward the apparatus of a simulation" (Petersen 28). This convergence is unsurprising given the entangled foundations of military and recreational forms of gaming and simulation. The advent of the computer age is massively underwritten by military financial and intellectual investments after World War II, and the cultural and technological work of simulation bears the mark of this origin forward into the twenty-first century.

FLIGHT SIMULATION AND THE TECHNOLOGIES OF PREEMPTION

The history of simulation technologies reaches back to the flight simulators of the early twentieth century. Originally designed in the context of military training, they came to play a significant role in the commercial development of recreational gaming as well. Simulating the experience of flight through a combination of sensory cues—including the agitation of dummy planes; the operations of responsive, realistic controls; and the use of projected moving imagery—these interactive simulators drew on and extended long-standing cultural fantasies of flight, harnessing them to the particular projects of targeting and war.

With the advent of aerial reconnaissance and combat in World War I, there emerged the need to train pilots in the mechanisms and routines of aerial warfare without putting lives (and planes) at risk. One of the earliest simulators to do so was the Link Trainer. The Link—devised by the son of an organ and piano manufacturer using the hydraulic pumps and bellows developed for the player piano—simulated the pitch and roll of an airborne craft (Halter 148). Named for its painted wood, the so-called blue box emphasized not the relationship of the pilot to the ground, as had earlier trainers, but the pilot's relationship to the plane's realistic cockpit controls. Originally created in 1929, the trainers caught on across the 1930s, first in a commercial market (including at the Midway at Coney Island, an early example of the relationship between flight simulators and amusement parks; Halter 149) and then in the context of military training. By World War II, blue boxes had become a standard means of aviation training.

After 1945, Link Trainers were updated to include screens on which images of varied environments appeared, at first through real-time video of intricate scale models and later through computerized scene generators (Crogan 42–43). The images were responsive to the trainer's interior controls. The miniaturized worlds over which the Link Trainers flew suggest the appeals of mastery and control out of which flight simulators grew, as well as the highly partial nature of the environments they modeled: attributes that pass onto the screens and digital worlds of videogames. The company itself survives to this day, as part of the Link Simulation & Training division of L3 Communications, an aerospace, surveillance, and communications company that contracts with the Pentagon and other government agencies (Halter 149).

In contrast to the early blue boxes, in the later Waller Flexible Gunnery Trainer, the role of the screen was central. This system was used to train aerial antiaircraft gunners while avoiding the risks and expense that airborne live-fire exercises would entail. Whereas the early Link Trainer miniaturized, the Waller sought to immerse. In the Waller, on which more than a million men trained during World War II, trainees aimed realistic dummy weapons at a wide five-part screen, onto which footage of attacking fighter planes was projected from five synchronized projectors (Taylor). When fired, the electronic guns shot a beam of light at the screen, which registered as a successful hit (or not) on the basis of specific calculations of weaponry, plane, flight trajectory, and angle of fire, such that the simulated process of targeting might most effectively mimic its real-world equivalent.

The Waller was carefully designed to maximize a viscerally immersive experience, with the domed screen curving around and above the trainee and sound effects such as engine noise and gunfire, as well as the weapon's simulated recoil, adding to the system's multisensory impact. Footage for the trainers featured aerial re-enactments of the attacking maneuvers of enemy fighter pilots, filmed from cameras mounted on the noses, tails, and turrets of planes, in positions usually occupied by the antiaircraft weapons themselves (Taylor 24). Thus, the Waller offered an image of war through a weapon's point of view. Although its curved widescreen was not commercialized until the appearance of Cinerama and CinemaScope in the early 1950s, the multisensory stimulations that the Waller delivered were likened by at least one trainee to "the feeling of being part of a Buck Rogers movie" (Taylor 27)—a comment that again underscores the cinema as a significant reference point for the simulated experience of war.

These early trainers demonstrate the crossover appeal of flight simulation, as military training overlaps with the attractions of the amusement park and the cinema. This conjunction is evident in an Army-sponsored exhibit at the popular Museum of Science and Industry in Chicago during the Vietnam War, in which patrons fired an electronic machine gun from the seat of a real "Huey" helicopter, aiming at "grass shacks" situated across a simulated Vietnamese river plain. The exhibit—which covered seventy-two hundred square feet of museum space—also included an armored personnel carrier that simulated movement over rugged terrain, an electronic antitank gun that could be fired at moving model tanks, and a shooting range, all demonstrating to "'stay-at-home America' . . . much of the actual killing equipment used in Vietnam," according to a museum spokesman ("New War"). The *Los Angeles Times* reviewed the exhibit under the headline, "New War Game in America: Shoot the Grass Shacks," and the *Chicago Tribune* announced "U.S. Weapons Put On Show," highlighting the military's direct engagement with the production of civilian recreation.

The attractions of virtual piloting—with its exhilarating mix of vertigo and control, coupling an embodied sense of risk with the seductions of a god's-eye view—continued to extend across training and entertainment contexts. Early networked games such as *Airflight* in the 1970s offered the thrill of aerial combat in an impressive range of simulated crafts. By the 1980s, as personal computers became a fixture in more homes across the country, MS-DOS-based PCs routinely shipped out with a copy of *Flight Simulator*. The game evolved into the successful *Microsoft Flight Simulator* series, "one of the longest-running, most influential, and successful game franchises of all time" (Halter 128). By the late 1990s, the Air Force borrowed back from commercial flight simulation, adapting the award-winning *Falcon 4.0* (Spectrum Holobyte, 1998) for use in training.

The overlapping practices and technologies of recreational and military simulation speak to their entangled origins in the evolution of computer technology itself. It was in the context of a wartime effort to create a more responsive and adaptive version of the Link Trainer—to produce a real-time antiaircraft training simulation responsive to pilot input, adaptable to the specific configurations of different planes and weapons, and able to more accurately mimic the trajectories of enemy fighters—that many of the components of digital technology were first developed (Halter 150). This effort, in combination with code breaking work during the war, is credited with inaugurating the computer age in the 1940s. During the Cold War, the military's heavy capital and intellectual investment in computing and electronics drove technological innovations through a web of governmental, industrial, and academic bodies funded or significantly subsidized by the Department of Defense (DoD). The efforts to refine the training capacity and the predictive precision of flight simulators and antiaircraft weaponry played a central role in the emergence of virtual reality and in the logic of preemption that shapes both videogames and war (Crogan).

The priorities that drove these innovations influence what comes after in direct and more subtle ways. Preemption entails a particular orientation, in which the anticipation of future outcomes shapes actions in the present (conditioning particular outcomes in the process). This orientation is marked by the context of conflict in which it developed: trying to anticipate the path of enemy aircraft to more effectively destroy it before it, by implication, destroys you. We can see how this logic governs many of the videogames that emerge as one legacy of these wartime technologies, in which the context of conflict is foundational. In videogames, as in the training simulations from which they evolve, skills are developed to manage and control anticipated violent futures. The orientation toward anticipated future violence and the increasing sense of competence and control that training regimes work to build form the basis of the vast and lucrative field of commercial interactive games.

Other key developments in the history of simulation include the first digital computer, the Electronic

Numerical Integrator And Computer (ENIAC), designed during World War II. As weapons systems evolved to deliver greater impacts from positions of greater physical remove, the requirements of accurate ballistics data grew increasingly complex. As in the recreational wargaming of chapter 1, these calculations eventually overwhelmed the capacities of human "computers" (as these mathematicians were called). ENIAC was designed to address this problem. After the war, it was believed that a broad range of social issues could be most effectively analyzed and addressed through the processing of mass quantities of statistical data, supported by the new technology of digital computing. The Cold War innovation of politico-military wargaming emerged in this context, incorporating not just data on troop movements and ballistics but a host of economic and diplomatic variables, translated into and computed as numerical values.

With the increased centrality of simulation to military strategy in the nuclear age—as atomic war could not be field-tested, even if atomic weapons could—the authority of combat experience came into tension with a new kind of expertise (Ghamari-Tabrizi, "Simulating" 163). As we have seen, combat experience "on the ground" is offered as a locus of truth and insight in live battle reenactments and screen-based simulations. In the institutions of defense, however, a class of virtual warriors was ascendant during the Cold War, alongside digital simulation. Game theory came to enjoy a new prominence in this period, as an approach that originated in the statistical framing of war was applied to business, science, and the analysis of social and political systems. While game theory imagines (and works to create) a world in which variables are calculable and actors rational, however, the persistent association of war with the unknowable hints at an underlying friction. As we have seen, the drive to simulate "real" war often reaches toward the more ineffable qualities of experience, and the conviction that real war remains outside the parameters of its representation drives the paradoxical quest to simulate war in ever more realistic ways.

The advent of networked communications was essential to the spread of interactive simulations. In allowing for shared virtual experience, digital networks provide the foundation for videogames and for the training for and waging of war as we have come to know it. Networking first emerged out of the desire to coordinate training within larger and more complex units: not just to train individual soldiers on specific weapons systems or in the context of particular battle scenarios but to train a vast coordinated force across land, air, and sea. Toward this purpose, in the 1980s, the DoD's Defense Advanced Research Projects Agency (DARPA) developed SIMNET, a simulation network in which hundreds of soldiers might train together in a shared virtual environment responsive in real time to user input. The system was first put to use in the Close Combat Tactical Trainer (CCTT), in which a realistic tank or Humvee interior was outfitted with screens, providing windows onto a shared virtual world; the sounds of engines, guns, and rotating turrets increased the simulation's immersive quality (Halter 153). Tank and armored vehicle units trained heavily with these simulators ahead of the Gulf War in 1991 (Crogan 14), a conflict that was wargamed extensively prior to its fighting (and again afterward to determine the effectiveness of the prewar training simulations; Lenoir and Lowood). Other examples of networked training include the Kernel Blitz 99 and Fort Irwin field exercises, discussed in chapter 1, in which the ability to link up and survey physically disparate spaces in real time was central.

Innovations such as SIMNET were part of a DoD effort to reduce the size and expense of the armed forces while increasing their flexibility and mobility. The idea of a networked military was central to the much-discussed concept of the Revolution in Military Affairs (RMA), which emphasizes the impact of information technologies on military structure, strategy, funding, and research, as well as on the nature of perceived threats. Networked trainers such as the CCTT entailed massive reductions in cost: while individual stand-alone tank trainers in the early 1980s could run over $6 million apiece, for instance, SIMNET trainers cost about $100,000 for each subsystem (though with many thousands of trainers in place, the program itself was still extremely costly; Halter 165).

Commercial recreational wargames emerge out of—and as part of—this history. Early networks such as SIMNET and its predecessors—alongside their military purpose—became seedbeds for exploration and recreation. A culture of so-called hackers devoted time and energy to the investigation of computer technology for its own sake, working on unofficial projects while in the employ of military-subsidized institutions. The interests and motivations of the hackers differed significantly—and sometimes explicitly—from those of the military establishment. Nonetheless, given their shared origins, while commercial videogames develop along their own trajectories, the fact that they continue to intersect and overlap with military projects and applications should in no way surprise us.

THE MILITARY-ENTERTAINMENT COMPLEX

The concept of the military-entertainment complex draws on President Dwight D. Eisenhower's parting admonition in January 1961 against the influence of a vast, new military-industrial complex that, if left unchecked, might threaten the foundational freedoms of democracy. This newer spin shares in the original's sense of foreboding. It speaks to the increasingly integrated funding, research, institutions, personnel, and products that link together the military and entertainment sectors, relationships we touched on in chapters 1 and 2 and trace further in the remainder of this chapter. James Der Derian's formulation of this complex as the "military-industrial-media-entertainment network," or MIME-NET, puts a suggestive emphasis on the mimetic impulses and virtual powers on which these relationships hinge.

The same technologies that supported the development of military simulations provided for an exploration of computer technologies in the interests of play. The storied history of *Spacewar!*, for instance—considered by many people to be the first videogame—begins in the DoD-funded Artificial Intelligence Laboratory at MIT. The impetus behind the game was a desire on the part of graduate students in the so-called Tech Model Railway Club to explore the capabilities of the new Programmed Data Processor 1 (PDP-1) "microcomputer" (which, unlike its behemoth contemporaries, took up "only 17 square feet of floor space," according to its operating manual; Halter 74). Developed in 1961–62, the game spread quickly to other laboratories and research centers; by 1963, the Computer Studies Department at

Stanford University had to strictly enforce its "No *Spacewar!* during business hours" policy in an attempt to mitigate its time-devouring popularity (Mead 16).

Spacewar! provides a link between the militarized technological innovations of the Cold War and the commercial videogame industry to follow. The game consists of two rocket ships with finite supplies of fuel and ammunition shooting projectiles at each other across a dark galactic void. Though the game was not motivated by any Pentagon directive, in its projectile-driven design, we can recognize the military context of targeting that originally shaped the development of computer technology. It was many hours playing *Spacewar!* that inspired Atari cofounder Nolan Bushnell in developing the first commercially successful arcade videogame, *Pong*. The breakout success of *Pong* in the early 1970s established beyond any lingering doubts the wide popularity and staying power of videogames as a form of commercial entertainment.

The Atari arcade tank gunner *BattleZone* (1980) is another landmark in commercial combat simulations. The game presents a spare, three-dimensional landscape sketched by thin green lines on a black screen: a large open field, ringed by distant mountains (and an erupting volcano), across which move enemy tanks and missiles (and the occasional UFO). The field is dotted with towering pyramids and cubes that serve as both obstacles and protection. The player navigates this space through the then-novel first-person perspective of a tank gunner, offering a new orientation to movement within a virtual world. The addition of a periscope on many of the cabinet versions of the game heightened the player's sense of identification with the position of the tank gunner (foreshadowing the heavy use of scopes and gun sights in the FPS to come). *BattleZone* was adapted for home computers across the 1980s, and numerous updated versions have appeared since, including a VR version in 2017 and *Battlezone: Gold Edition* for console and PC in 2018.

By the late 1970s, weapons-training simulations were common across all branches of the military, and arcade games were one source that the Army reviewed for potential usefulness. In addition to targeting arcades as recruitment sites—in search of "joystick warriors" already acclimated to the technologies of simulated combat—in 1980, the Army approached Atari about designing a version of *BattleZone* for use as a trainer for the Bradley Infantry Fighting Vehicle. Although the Atari designer Ed Rotberg did so only under duress, the resulting *Bradley Trainer* provides another example of the fluid status of combat simulation as both training and entertainment. Popular culture of the 1980s highlighted this overlap as well, in movies such as *WarGames* (dir. Badham, 1983) and *The Last Starfighter* (dir. Castle, 1984) and the novel *Ender's Game* (1985), in which simulated combat merges with the playing out of violent conflicts in the real world. In the context of military training, the impulse to tap the militarized currents of popular commercial entertainment in the service of more specific military aims would prove an enduring one. In these exchanges, the idea of fun is not understood as anomalous to the serious business of war but rather as an augmentation of the process of training for it.

At the same time, games explored more fantastical preoccupations: their distance from, rather than overlap with, the real. In 1992, the groundbreaking *Wolfenstein 3D* (Activision, 1992) inaugurated many enduring conventions of the FPS. Here the player, as the American spy, William "B.J." Blazkowicz, fights off Nazi soldiers and guard dogs (and later more varied adversaries, including zombie mutants and a chain-gun-wielding Adolf Hitler) while moving through the rooms of a German castle-cum-prison. *Wolfenstein 3D* includes many features that would become FPS hallmarks: an emphasis on fast action; the appearance of an onscreen weapon marking the presence of the player's avatar; a "heads-up display" (HUD) set apart from the virtual space of the gameworld and indicating resources such as health, ammunition, weapons, and equipment; and progressively difficult "levels" of gameplay, with each culminating in the appearance of a particularly formidable adversary.

It was id Software's 1993 release, *Doom*, that solidified the conventions of the FPS and linked fantastical gameplay back to its militarized origins. The game—in which the player, armed with an unprecedented array of weapons, must navigate through a labyrinthine series of rooms while warding off a horde of alien demons, zombies, and monsters—capitalized on technological advances in both sound and image to render a more viscerally engaging and navigable virtual space. The ability to move through a three-dimensional space with increased speed and precision created a more immersive relationship to the onscreen image as a habitable environment. *Doom*'s success helped to institutionalize a particular structure of gameplay, in which the player's position is defined at once through its violent agency and its constant vulnerability: a conjunction foundational to the FPS.

The free online distribution of *Doom*'s first levels and the subsequent release of its level editor encouraged a vast and unprecedented array of player customizations, opening up a new era of user-created modifications. Follow-up games such as *Quake* (id Software, 1996) maintained the structure of gameplay while focusing on multiplayer modes, as the internet established itself as a central feature of the videogame industry. Other successful FPS soon followed, including *Unreal* (Epic Games, 1998), which supplied the game engine for *America's Army*, discussed shortly; *Half-Life* (Valve, 1998), which introduced scripted in-game sequences, increasing the player's sense of immersion through narrative and character-based identification; and *Halo* (Bungie, 2001). *Half-Life* became the basis for the tremendously successful mod *Counter-Strike* (Valve Software, 2000), a terrorism-themed multiplayer FPS that became, by late 1999, the most popular online game to date.

One of the most notorious *Doom* mods was *Marine Doom* (1996), based on *Doom II* (id Software, 1994) and developed by the Marine Corp's Modeling and Simulation Management Office as a training simulation. The game emerged in response to shifts in the military at the end of the Cold War: shrinking budgets and a cost-cutting directive encouraging use of commercial off-the-shelf products (COTS) for training purposes; and shrinking troop levels and an increased reliance on reservists, who required distance training from their home bases. In a notorious bit of frugality, it cost the Marine Corps $49.95 to purchase and modify *Doom II* (Platoni). Instead of blasting away demons with a plasma rifle, players of *Marine Doom* battled enemy troops with authentic military weapons through brick bunkers, foxholes, and fields littered with tactical wire. In contrast to the original game, *Marine Doom* featured a four-man team controlled by up to two players and was intended as fireteam training. Though never part of an official training program, the game was distributed widely on government computers, where Marines were encouraged to play under conditions that would best mimic the physical and emotional stress of war (Halter 169). The game was considered a training success, helping to invigorate the military's interest in COTS.

Across the 1990s, the flow of traffic between military training simulations and recreational videogames became more regularized, driven by the commercial investment in selling military "authenticity" and the military investment in more advanced commercial game engines. The movement ran in both directions: *Real War* (Rival Interactive, 2001)—a terrorism-themed strategy game first developed for the Joint Chiefs of Staff as *Joint Force Employment* and subsequently released to the public—tried to capitalize on the appeal of military authenticity, amplifying this marketing angle during its release in September 2001 (Stahl, *Militainment* 94). Like *Marine Doom* and *Falcon 4.0*, other commercial games were repurposed as military trainers, including *Jane's Fleet Command* (Electronic Arts, 1999); *Operation Flashpoint* (Bohemia Interactive Studio, 2001), adapted as *Virtual Battlespace*; *Tom Clancy's Rainbow Six: Rogue Spear* (Ubisoft, 1999), employed to support Army MOUT training; and a modified version of *Microsoft's Flight Simulator,* among numerous others.

By the early years of the war on terror, the merchandising of military realness reached a zenith, with games such as *SOCOM: U.S. Navy SEALS* (2002), developed in consultation with the U.S. Naval Special Warfare Command; and Kuma Reality Games' *Kuma/War* (2004), a subscription series of playable missions based on recent military actions and accompanied by Kuma-produced cable-style "newscasts." In one particularly bald attempt to market an association with real-world violence, in March 2003, Sony applied for the trademark phrase "shock and awe" for use as a game title the day after the U.S. government opened its much-anticipated "shock and awe" bombing of Iraq (Stahl, *Militainment* 101). Electronic Arts captured the spirit of this era with a semantically slippery new slogan released on the eve of the U.S. invasion: "Real War. Real Games."

The relationship between military and commercial combat simulations took institutional form in 1999 with the launch of the Institute for Creative Technologies (ICT), housed at the University of Southern California in Los Angeles. The institute emerged out of government-convened simulation workshops in the mid-1990s, organized to increase collaboration between military and entertainment sectors and attended by an impressive list of Hollywood brass, tech executives, game designers, computer scientists, and military personnel. With an initial DoD grant of $45 million (and another $135 million in 2011), the stated purpose of the ICT was to bring the military together with Hollywood and the game industry—alongside academics, toy manufacturers, and other players in the entertainment sector—to create "synthetic experiences so compelling that participants react as if they are real" (or, more specifically, in the words of one spokesman, "to create veterans who've never seen combat"; Dyer-Witheford and de Peuter 102). The simulation technologies developed at the ICT support applications across a range of contexts, including theme parks, videogames, military trainers, and movies. Attesting to the increased centrality of simulation to U.S. warfare, the ICT was quickly followed by the establishment of other DoD simulation offices.

In combat simulations, visceral and sensory cues alone are not enough to provoke full involvement on the part of the trainee: emotional involvement and the story elements that prompt it are also central. This was a key impetus for the ICT's formation, for while military simulations did an excellent job rendering weapons and tactics, these training applications lacked the story and character development that made virtual worlds credible and engaging. Thus, while the military might produce highly "authentic" simulations, in comparison to their commercial counterparts, they were felt to be less realistic. By amplifying users' emotional engagement, cinematic conventions were understood to render the virtual world more believable: ultimately (and as we saw in chapter 2), to look and feel more "real," a simulation needed to look and feel more like a movie. In celebrating the advent of the ICT, military brass referenced the Omaha Beach sequence from *Saving Private Ryan* as a model of realism through which training might be "enhanced" (Ghamari-Tabrizi, "Convergence" 164).

Among the projects of the ICT is the award-winning *Full Spectrum Warrior* (Pandemic Studios, 2004), a real-time squad-based tactical game developed to tap both military and commercial markets. The game is set in the fictional though nonetheless familiar Middle Eastern nation of Zekistan—refuge to Taliban and Al-Qaeda forces that have fled their native lands under U.S. attack—and is focused on the overthrow of the Zekistani dictator Al-Afad. The game's commercial release in April 2003, one month after the United States' invasion of Iraq, was encouraged by market research suggesting an audience receptive to gaming contemporary real-world conflicts (Stahl, *Militainment* 96). Highlighting the game's merger of military and commercial interests, its website originally included a link to the Army's recruiting site. Following in the Army's footsteps, the Marines developed a training game of their own, *Close Combat: First to Fight,* which was released in 2005 as part of the longer-running *Close Combat* series.

Full Spectrum Warrior was widely celebrated for its realism, as signified both through its graphics and through its official connection with the military. The differences between the commercial and military versions, however, are instructive to note. The former features higher sound quality and an evocative musical score, more detailed rendering of the physical environment, and cinematic cut scenes outlining the individuated soldiers of the Alpha and Bravo teams, whose movements the player controls: a familiar "band of brothers" adhering to the cinematic conventions of "militarized multiculturalism" (Dyer-Witheford and de Peuter 108). In contrast, the military version (which could also be unlocked on the commercial Xbox release) is aesthetically much more spare and eschews cut scenes and individual characterizations. It features more civilians (notoriously lacking in most commercial games) and is widely recognized as a more challenging game (Dyer-Witheford and de Peuter 113): in both respects, more accurate to actual combat scenarios. In contrast to the great success of the commercial version, however, the military one was considered largely a failure due to its inadequate realism.

In other projects, the ICT has worked to produce hybrid or "mixed reality" environments, in which virtual and material worlds merge at the level of experience. One such is FlatWorld, a VR environment composed of digital flats and real-time graphics, inspired by the *Star Trek* holodeck (and spearheaded by the ICT executive director, Richard Lindheim, for many years a *Star Trek* producer). The goal of the project was to create a mobile, cost-effective trainer through which a wide variety of real-world environments might be effectively simulated. In contrast to virtual "shoot houses" in which trainees fire at holographic enemies, FlatWorld offers a training simulation unencumbered by head-mount displays, in an effort to produce a more seamless immersion. Though located at the cutting-edge of simulation technologies, FlatWorld recalls the moving panoramas and cycloramas of the nineteenth century, which frequently featured scenes of battle and, like FlatWorld, foregrounded three-dimensional objects against virtual landscapes to construct an immersive (though not yet interactive) mixed-reality environment (as in the "Battle of Gettysburg" cyclorama, still on view today). In FlatWorld, users interact with material objects as they move through virtual spaces, their visual, auditory, and tactile experience augmented by 4-D elements such as temperature, odor, and humidity. The use of 4-D elements features also in the ICT's *Virtual Iraq* and *Virtual Afghanistan* projects: adaptations of *Full Spectrum Warrior* developed to help treat soldiers suffering from posttraumatic stress, in which—to recover from war—soldiers revisit the same virtual world in which they trained for it.

In addition to the ICT, other DARPA-funded sites include Team Orlando, a "co-located collaboration" between military, academic, and industry partners. Here the proximity of entertainment giants such as Disney and Universal Studios alongside defense contractors and the University of Central Florida's Institute for Simulation and Training has made for an unprecedented concentration of money and personnel focused broadly on the projects of modeling and simulation. According to the alliance's promotional video "They Are Ready," Team Orlando aims to produce "training that feels and even smells like the real thing" (Team Orlando). This assertion immediately follows a close-up of a simulated bloody leg stump, suggesting the persistent association between realness and onscreen gore.

Among the military bodies gathered under the Team Orlando umbrella is the Army's Simulation, Training, and Instrumentation Command (PEO STRI). PEO STRI hosted the annual Defense GameTech conference in Orlando to advocate for the military use of videogames and game technologies (Mead) and contracted with the commercial software company Bohemia Interactive Simulations to produce *Virtual Battlespace,* now the Army's official simulation platform and currently in its third iteration, *VBS3* (BISim, 2014). As detailed on the BISim website, *VB3* is a customizable "virtual sandbox": a highly adaptable "desktop training package" with over fourteen thousand different weapons, vehicles, and character models, equipped for a vast range of training scenarios and mission rehearsals (BIS). By tapping into other DoD systems, the game links its virtual environments and gameplay mechanics to their real-world counterparts, providing for the simulation of specific combat areas whose size and detail exceed the normal conventions of the FPS. Correspondences extend to the capacities of the individualized avatar, whose size, speed, and weapons proficiency fluctuate in accordance with the soldier's own real-world stats (Lenoir and Caldwell 86).

In offering graphics and gameplay to rival those of popular commercial games, *VB3* takes its cue from the storied success of the FPS *America's Army,* developed by the Army in response to record-low recruitments in the late 1990s. With an initial budget of $8 million, the game was designed with the explicit intent of reaching a videogame-playing demographic of boys and young men, officially to educate them about the Army and unofficially to encourage their enlistment. It was based on a recognition of the shared interfaces linking videogames and combat and an interest in tapping the aptitudes and proficiencies of players in this regard. Extensive data tracking was included within the game in an attempt to facilitate the pairing of players with real-world military pathways if and when they surfaced at the recruitment office.

Using the most sophisticated game engine available and distributed free online (through a website that included a direct link to the Army's recruiting site, goarmy.com), *America's Army* was rolled out with tremendous success on July 4, 2002, tallying four hundred thousand downloads in the first day alone (Lenoir and Caldwell 74). For the release of *America's Army: Special Forces* the following year, the Army staged a $500,000 no-holds-barred spectacle at the annual E3 expo, complete with machine-gun-wielding soldiers rappelling down from a flock of Black Hawk helicopters. More versions of the game followed, including console, cell phone, and arcade editions, as well as adaptations for training purposes. Overall, the project was considered a recruitment triumph. In an Army survey conducted in 2007, 29 percent of sixteen- to twenty-four-year-olds in the United

States indicated having contact with the game in the previous six months (Andersen and Kurti 49).

As compared to other FPS, *America's Army* represented some significant deviations. Unlike *Doom* and *Half-Life,* which had generated a wealth of mods, *America's Army* did not allow for player modifications. Instead, the game stuck closely to its official script, staking its appeal on the idea of its authenticity and incorporating official Army values and codes of conduct into the structure of gameplay. As ever, the notion of authenticity applied selectively. Military materiel was rendered with great precision, and the game's training levels were modeled closely on the Army's own Fort Benning. Combat played out on conspicuously civilian-free maps, however, and death came quickly with a puff of red and the evaporation of casualties from the screen. While the Army cited its Teen rating and moral objection to the sensationalization of violence, in the context of a recruitment game sold on the basis of its authenticity, the failure to render the messy physical and moral entanglements of war supported the game's more marketable image of military service as both noble and fun.

In merging recruitment and entertainment, the Army Game Project of which *America's Army* is the flagship recalls the double status of the early flight simulators as both military trainers and amusement-park attractions. This resonance is particularly evident in the example of the Virtual Army Experience (VAE), a mobile combat simulator that traveled to large public events such as state fairs, air shows, and NASCAR races between 2007 and 2010. At the VAE, after waiting in a long line and undergoing a pre-mission "briefing" by military personnel, visitors could take up seats in life-size Humvees and Black Hawks, to engage with realistic weapons in multiplayer combat appearing on huge screens around them. Like *America's Army*, the VAE worked to situate the visceral thrills of the amusement-park ride and the satisfactions of the shooting gallery within a larger narrative of honor, heroism, and service. In a debriefing after, one of the "Real Heroes" featured on the game's website emerged to speak about his own army experiences (and hand out one of the Real Hero action figures modeled on him). Recruiters were on hand as visitors exited the attraction to supply information to anyone interested in upgrading from simulation to enlistment. Open from 2008 to 2010, the $13 million Army Experience Center made the attractions of the VAE a permanent fixture at the Franklin Mills Mall in Philadelphia, where consumers might integrate interactive wargaming into their regular routines of leisure and shopping, under the watchful eyes of Army recruiters.

FIRST-PERSON SHOOTERS

War-themed videogames are a large, diverse category, encompassing flight and tank simulators, first-person shooters, turn-based and real-time strategy games, and massively multiplayer online role-playing games. Strategy games mobilize the commanding perspective of *kriegs-spiel* and its descendants, in which one plays a conflict rather than a character, controlling multiple units rather than an individual avatar. In the FPS, in contrast, the bigger picture tends to fall away through identification with an embedded perspective (though this framework may be restored through cut scenes between levels). In its invitation to enter into a visceral identification with simulated combat, the FPS is a key medium of somatic war, linking up to cinema and television, as well as to the live reenactment traditions of chapter 1.

We might follow Chris Suellentrop's lead and consider if such games would be more usefully described as second- rather than first-person shooters. This nomenclature captures how the games hail a "you," inviting identification with the onscreen avatar as a representation and extension of the player him- or herself. Recognizing the centrality of this "you" helps us appreciate the function of games as recruitment (though we still must ask to what they recruit us). Strategy games too might be considered as offering a distinct form of this second-person perspective, positioning "you" as a commander or even a god, with a broad overview of action and the ability to control vast numbers of troops and materiel. This more flexible second-person classification allows us to make sense of military shooters that enable shuttling between first- and third-person perspectives, inviting an alternating identification with "you" entangled in combat action and "you" positioned strategically above it. In relation to the drone's-eye view mobilized in FPS franchises such as *Battlefield* and *Call of Duty,* a second-person perspective highlights how the game temporarily aligns "you" with the weaponized stare of the drone.

The FPS is the most popular and lucrative videogame genre. *Call of Duty,* for instance, is the most successful franchise of all time and has repeatedly achieved launches unrivaled in any medium across the history of mass entertainment; as of 2016, its games reportedly exceeded $15 billion in worldwide sales. Within the category of the FPS, the texture and experience of gameplay can differ significantly across franchises, titles, and platforms, driven by different game engines and varying weapons, tactics, maps, and missions, as well as a host of other contextual factors. Nonetheless a few basic conventions persist: the FPS at its most fundamental level is defined by a subjective in-game perspective, the basic mission of moving through space and the regular encounter of obstacles impeding this movement, and the clearing of these obstacles through the act of shooting. It is in the FPS that Paul Virilio's insight into the relationship of technologies of sight to technologies of destruction finds its most compelling popular form, as the eye takes on "the function of a weapon" (4).

More than any other genre, the FPS highlights the lineage of videogames in military simulation technologies oriented toward the anticipation and control of the future through preemptive violence. Like the first simulators and the early games that developed out of them, in the FPS, the gamer's relationship to the screen is defined through targeting. Whether against the galactic sky of *Spacewar!*, across the abstract landscape of *Battlezone*, or through the labyrinth of *Doom*, the control of a weapon secures identification with the image. The gamer appears onscreen *as* the gun and confirms his or her ability to impact the onscreen environment through control *of* the gun, the use of which cements the relationship between a tactile interaction with the controller and a sense of presence and agency within the gameworld.

This agency, however, is highly limited. According to one player, the excitement of military shooters comes from "taking a chaotic situation like [war] and putting an order to it that I command" (Payne 184). Indeed, shooters proffer the satisfactions of mastery, competence, and control as primary attractions. Historical gaming might be understood as a way to ascribe meaning to the messy contingencies of lived experience; and future-oriented games likewise structure unknowables into familiar forms and pleasures. But while games construct a sense of agency, they also constrain it: game mechanics and pathways are programmed in advance, and choice is often highly circumscribed. The virtual environments of the FPS are shaped by specific kinds of violent scenarios, and gameplay works to condition goals and actions in particular ways: some orientations to gameplay are rewarded with increased resources and access to higher levels and bonus materials; others are not. Games are differentiated and marketed in part based on the affective experiences they deliver; thus, maintaining gameplay within specific parameters becomes one investment in the branding of a successful franchise.

The conventions of the FPS shifted across the first decades of the twenty-first century. Following Steven Spielberg's groundbreaking *Medal of Honor* (*MoH*; DreamWorks Interactive, 1999), the genre moved away from fantastical scenarios toward a historical realism focused particularly around World War II. Game sales spiked after 9/11 amid the steady national drumbeat toward war, suggesting perhaps both jingoism and the appeal of virtual mastery and control in a world that had come, for many Americans, unmoored from its founding certainties. As the war on terror dragged on, *Medal of Honor* and its successors—including the early releases of storied franchises such as *Battlefield, Brothers in Arms,* and *Call of Duty*—offered the excitement of virtual combat within a familiar universe of good and evil, providing violent action with a moral clarity missing from the protracted occupations of Afghanistan and Iraq.

With the release of *Battlefield 2* in 2005, followed by the unprecedented success of *Call of Duty 4: Modern Warfare* (Infinity Ward) in 2007, the FPS turned its primary attention from World War II to focus on just past or future possible conflicts in the forever war on terror. These games amplify the preemptive impulse of all videogames, as the gaming of near-future conflicts helps to shape the imagination of threat in the present. In simulating conflicts based on present-day political and military tensions, priorities, and presumptions, the FPS aligns with contemporary beliefs and values about the nature of war fighting and the character of the enemy. In helping to shape expectations of what future war will become, "these games don't just mirror the future of warfare but also help to produce it" (Lenoir and Caldwell 143).

One aspect of the realist turn in the FPS is the shifting representation of the enemy away from zombies and aliens and toward human "opposing forces" (although, true to form, the undead persist in zombie modes and spin-offs). In the age of *Doom*, the violence of the FPS was a focus of significant controversy, associated with its real-world counterpart. With the alignment of the realist FPS with both historical battles and contemporary military doctrine, however, the controversy over violent gameplay and its implications largely falls away (Voorhees).

Akin to the Hollywood protagonists of chapter 2, the subject position constructed by the FPS is defined through both agency and vulnerability: like the sniper on the rooftop or the hero in his tank, the player-protagonist of the FPS is at once supremely powerful and perpetually vulnerable. The genre's focus on special operations forces amplifies this construction, highlighting small, elite units of highly trained men, inevitably outnumbered but endowed with an arsenal of high-tech weapons and equipment. These figures maintain the status of the underdog (and the virtue this position conventionally entails) while asserting superior strength and readiness. Like the action heroes they resemble, they are at once vulnerable and invincible (Eagle). For Gulf War games such as the tactical shooter *Conflict: Desert Storm* (Pivotal, 2002), this formula presents a challenge, requiring designers to bracket the overwhelming force of U.S. airstrikes (Thomson 95). But by the 2010s, the FPS's increasing emphasis on counterterrorist scenarios, covert operations, targeted killings, and high-tech weaponry aligns strikingly well with official military doctrine, helping to legitimize a new American way of war (Lenoir and Caldwell; Thomson).

REALISM IN VIDEOGAMES

In interactive simulations as in their live and screen-based kin, the values of realness and authenticity are central. As computer memory gets cheaper and processing speeds faster, gameworlds support more fluid and varied movements through more textured and responsive environments. While the real-world psychics of movement, light, and impact are applied to gameworlds and mechanics, the concept of realness itself continues to operate in particular and selective ways. As we have seen, in military shooters, realness adheres to cinematic conventions of spectacle and action and to familiar story forms and characters. It also adheres to the precise rendering of graphic and sonic detail (of military hardware in particular), fidelity with real-world physics (of ballistics in particular), correspondence with period-specific tactics and environments, responsiveness of game mechanics, and sophistication of AI components. While attention to weapons and vehicles or to the physics of high-speed impacts may be meticulous, however, other aspects of combat experience—or, in historical games, of particular conflicts—are rendered much more loosely, baldly revised, or ignored altogether. The experiences of war that do not get simulated tend to fall outside the cultural imagination of "real war" in a paradoxical, reinforcing loop—in which (to put it crudely) realness is only real to the extent that it gets faked—ultimately limiting our cultural capacity to reckon fully with either the experience of war or with its costs.

Medal of Honor was the first game to combine a new level of graphic detail with wargaming's traditional focus on historical authenticity. Spielberg, who faced considerable skepticism about the appeal of historical gameplay, brought to *MoH* the same zeal for authenticity that animated *Saving Private Ryan*. In *MoH* and its successors, graphical realism—the rendering of a highly detailed physical world that corresponds in appearance to the material world—meets up with historical realism. These different modes of realism support and augment each other, as the simulation of historical conflicts from familiar perspectives adds credibility to the virtual world, even as the sophisticated level of visual and sonic detail props up the "realness" of the historical material. As citizens and as consumers, we tend to believe in those representations that align with what we already hold to be true: an image, newscast, or film that echoes our values and beliefs is one we accept most readily as realistic. In this way, different appeals to the real can function as a feedback loop: the "sensorial clutter of nondigital existence" (Halter xiii) adds credence to the gameworld; while the alignment of this world with an already accepted truth (whether of the nature of a particular historical conflict or of the merit of contemporary military doctrine) supports the realism of visual, auditory, and other perceptual cues.

Through this symbiosis, the patently unrealistic aspects of gameplay and the gameworlds that support it are caught up in the net of the real. Military shooters, for instance, introduce the exhilarations of cinematic fast action and violence into perceptually familiar surrounds, offering these as key elements of the real war they construct. Violence is rendered through and in relation to the specific dynamics and potentials of weapons, detailed knowledge of which operates as its own kind of capital within both games and the communities they foster. Games work within their realist frame to naturalize a particular imagination of war (and many forms of violence remain outside this frame). Key features of this imagination include heroic narratives of unlikely achievement; the removal of long periods of waiting and boredom and mundane, inglorious tasks; inattention to the long-term aftermaths of war; and the general absence of civilians and, with them, of moral ambiguity. The latter two return with a vengeance in the notorious "No Russian" level of *Call of Duty: Modern Warfare 2* (Infinity Ward, 2009), in which the player is impelled to massacre civilians in an airport to maintain undercover status. Such deviations are usually marketed as such, however, underscoring established conventions in contrast.

Amplifying the gore factor became one means of product differentiation in the crowded field of the FPS starting in the early 2000s, in games that adhered to proven elements of the genre in other respects. In *Soldier of Fortune* (Raven Software, 2000), for example, violence is diversified through the graphic visualization of twenty-six distinct "gore zones," each one triggering a unique representation of bodily violation, dismemberment, and disintegration. In franchises whose brand identity revolves around the representation of carnage, realist claims are staked on the degree of visual and sonic detail through which onscreen violence is rendered: a formulation we recognize from contemporary cinema. As in cinema, the impulse is both realist and highly stylized.

When *America's Army* was released in 2002, it deviated from the trend toward graphic violence, staking its realist claims on its Army provenance rather than the rendering of what bullets can do to bodies. Similarly, and in stark contrast to the film that inspired it, the casualties that litter the beaches of Normandy in *Medal of Honor* are clean and tidy: free of blood, missing limbs, or organs oozing into the sand. As in *America's Army,* when hit, soldiers gently collapse and vanish from the screen. *Call of Duty: WWII* (Sledgehammer Games, 2017), however, offers a direct homage to *Saving Private Ryan,* complete with splattered "camera lens," beaches washed with blood, exploding brains, and graphic dismemberment. In contrast to *Soldier of Fortune,* the violence of *Call of Duty* has not attracted particular attention, suggesting how sensationalism itself can be naturalized by the familiar framework of historical realism. Instead, the game has been celebrated as a stellar example of visual and sound design, immersing the player in a gameworld at once beautiful and harrowing.

In general then, war-themed games use different modes of authentication to construct and market their relationship to the real. These include official military involvement and consultation, and employment of retired officers, soldiers, and veterans of specific conflicts as subject-matter experts (though tellingly subject-matter experts can also include Hollywood personnel). In tactical real-time games such as *Men of War: Assault Squad* (Digitalmindsoft, 2011), the rigor of gameplay itself may provide an authenticating function, augmenting the visual and sonic intricacies of the gameworld and connoting something of the "real" of war. Making videogame combat feel more "real" has often meant increasing the speed and intensity of gameplay, enriching the visual and sonic texture of gameworlds, and aligning characters and themes with both Hollywood movies and contemporary military doctrine. Entering into this world feels real, paradoxically, to the extent that it feels like entering into a movie.

The cinematic functions as a primary and a varied mode of authentication. We recognize it in the conventions of sensational realism, in familiar icons, settings, themes, and characters (often voiced by Hollywood actors), and in the crucial work of soundtrack in generating both the "realness" and the affective richness of videogames. We can note it, too, in the persistently filmic language through which we understand and describe games themselves (so that the innovative immersive style of *God of War* [Santa Monica Studio, 2018] is experienced as a "40-hour steadycam shot," for instance; Tran). Transmedia properties such as *Star Wars: Battlefront* and others that move between videogames and Hollywood further cement this relationship, one that is emphasized in the games and in the promotional discourse that surrounds them.

The cinematic (and the televisual) are also present in noninteractive cut scenes (also called cinematics) that introduce and play between levels. Cut scenes may include live-action and prerendered sequences, documentary clips and newsreels, sophisticated infographics, or—in earlier games—a still image accompanied by text and audio. They provide backstories and broader historical frameworks, outline missions and gameplay elements, introduce and develop characters, and grant a sense of linear narrative progress to gameplay. While cut scenes may seem marginal (and can often be skipped), the most lauded and successful games integrate immersive action and violence with a strong sense of story and character, functions conventionally carried by cut scenes.

The context of a larger mission that story elements construct frames the visceral qualities of gameplay to produce a compelling sense of the real (and we might say something similar of *Saving Private Ryan,* in which the realism of combat chaos is not contradicted but supported by the conventional narrative that surrounds it). Even in games such as *Medal of Honor: Allied Assault* (2015, Inc., 2002) that eschew cut scenes and deliver mission objectives in-game, story elements tether the energies of gameplay along tightly constructed lines. Especially in single-player campaign modes, these elements sharpen but also contain interaction with the virtual world, directing affective investments in particular ways and situating images of violence within familiar narrative contexts. By tapping into established conventions of story and character, training simulations and commercial games alike activate the expectations of specific generic forms: in the case of military shooters, those of Hollywood action melodrama (Eagle). As we have seen, doing so does not make these simulations seem less realistic but rather more so.

Thus, the realism of these videogames depends at once on their proximity to everyday experience and their distance from it. Violent impacts are rendered in accordance with real-world ballistics, and the "sensorial clutter" of highly detailed environments corresponds to our visual experience in many ways. Yet military shooters, in their sensationalism and their aesthetics, stake out their distinction from daily life. These aesthetics are often described as "hyperreal" (or, in the case of *Call of Duty*, "epic realism") in an effort to underscore the simulated quality of "more than" that defines them. Even the photorealistic qualities of game environments enable a vision that is something more and other than everyday perception, heightening our ability to apprehend in detail the many-textured surfaces that surround us. This enhanced vision is constituted through digital rendering and extended in-game through military prosthetics such as infrared optics and satellite and radar feeds. As in the cinema, it is technology itself that is on display in the rendering of these gameworlds and mechanics, as videogames assert what "real" war looks like while highlighting its active construction as such.

The artist and critic Jordan Crandall has suggested that, as technologies of vision enable more precise and detailed views of the world around us, we tend to attribute authenticity less to our own perceptual faculties than to these technologies themselves, a point we might consider in relation to the enhanced vision of military shooters. Crandall highlights how a logic of preemption shapes our vision in contexts that become "not about seeing, but about tracking: detecting an object with unprecedented accuracy, pinpointing it precisely in time and space, understanding how it moves, and predicting its future position" (217): a description that might fit a drone or, equally well, a videogame.

BACK TO THE BATTLEFIELD

Military and civilian modes of war gaming have long bled into each other, as we have seen, and the way we game wars impacts and reflects the way we fight them. In the age of interactive war, this convergence is more apparent than ever. Shared technologies, interfaces, and controls provide the means of recreation and training as well as war waging; in 2000, for instance, the Japanese government applied export controls to the PlayStation2 on the basis of its resemblance to a weapons guidance system, a point that underscores these shared technologies (Stahl, *Militainment* 91). Soldiers habituated to the mechanisms of simulated combat enter into real-world conflicts that reproduce these mechanisms, as the augmented realities and hybrid environments in which they trained extend to encompass the battlefield itself. In both training and combat, embodied experience is shaped through a combination of material and virtual inputs and conditions.

The ascendance of interactive war traces back to the Cold War developments discussed at the opening of this chapter. By the 1980s, the field exercises of chapter 1 were already heavily digitized and networked, relying on an array of interactive technologies to link overhead surveillance by camera, radar, and satellite to central command points as well as to screen-equipped tanks and helmet-mounted displays. Soldiers (outfitted with cameras, screens, and small computer packs alongside their uniforms and weapons) were mobilized as digital data collection points, and data fed back to a centralized command guided battlefield strategy with the assistance of computer-generated analysis. Later initiatives such as Future Force Warrior continued to work toward the integration of soldiers into battlefield networks, with access to a wealth of real-time data through wearable, voice-activated displays, among other innovations.

Although the Future Force Warrior was not fielded as such, in modeling future weapons and communications technologies, such initiatives supply popular culture with a rich imagination of combat in near and distant futures. The close relationship between military and entertainment sectors keeps game designers up-to-date on new and future weapons systems, which in turn shape the virtual worlds of gameplay. In *Tom Clancy's Ghost Recon: Advanced Warfighter* (Ubisoft, 2006), for instance, the player operates as a "high-tech, decision-making node in an interconnected, cybernetic weapons system," mobilizing an "Integrated Warfighter System" based on the Future Force Warrior (Payne 104). At the same time, the new modes of attention and perception conditioned by the networked, screen-based technologies of contemporary war are familiar from videogame play: the modern soldier—like the gamer—must integrate a rich field of two-dimensional data displays with the immersive field of battle action, pivoting between informational and interactional modes of perception.

Drones such as the Predator, Global Hawk, and Reaper provide the most prominent example of the contemporary relationship of interactive, screen-based simulation to war. As noted, drone interfaces are self-consciously modeled on commercial game consoles in an attempt to harness pilots' comfort and familiarity with videogame-style controls. The massive increase in drone-led warfare across the first decade of the twenty-first century was staggering, with the number of drones owned by the Pentagon increasing from 167 to 7,500 between 2002 and 2010, and their budget increasing from $284 million to $3.3 billion between 2000 and 2010 (Lenoir and Caldwell 40). By 2016, in the face of this precipitous increase, the military started hiring private contractors to fill the shortage in drone pilots (Schmidt). Drone strikes have escalated and their targets have expanded under the Trump administration, although their operations are shrouded in increasing layers of secrecy (Parks; Rosenthal and Schulman).

While the relationship of realness and simulation seems to be shifting in these contexts, on the ground the material realities of war continue, both altered and in some important senses unchanged by new weapons technologies. To those who are their targets, the force and impact of missiles and bombs still arrive messy and chaotic, rending worlds and communities as they rip apart bodies, buildings, and terrain. Those living under the persistent whine of the drones endure the stress and uncertainty that constant surveillance and the ever-present threat of violence condition. At an increasing remove from the scene of violence, pilots and analysts guide these crafts and evaluate their missions from many thousands of miles away, warehoused in the deserts of Nevada and New Mexico or the fields of North Dakota.

The bracketing of immediate bodily threat and harm has not eliminated the psychological damage of war in these contexts, however, as drone pilots appear to suffer from anxiety, depression, and suicidal thoughts at a rate equal to other pilots (Dao). Interestingly, it is the remove of drone piloting from the visceral, embodied thrill of high speed and sensation that has itself been identified as one root cause of stress on the job. While profoundly lacking in equivalence to the stress of living as or within a targeted community, the high incidence of posttraumatic stress among drone pilots nonetheless indicates how the battlefield extends to their position at the console. Meanwhile, for every "soldier-technician" for whom the means of fighting and simulating war are nearly identical, for the grunts on the ground, packs get heavier in the context of networked war, and the experiences of heat, weight, thirst, and fatigue remain much the same (Van Creveld 190).

The paradoxical quest for realistic simulations of war has always been a complicated one, underwritten by real military priorities and commitments and carrying real-world consequences but haunted also by a collective sense that the real of war remains forever out of reach: that the virtual can replicate or even overwhelm it but loses out to it inevitably in the end. In the operations of simulation, there is always a remainder, whether in the complex unfolding of contingent events in the world, which cannot be adequately modeled or predicted, or in our sense that something resides in material, embodied experience that cannot be mediated through screens or digital technologies. In closing out this volume more or less where we began it—with the question of war and its practice—we must ask ourselves what, if anything, has changed about this relationship. In an age of hybrid environments and mixed realities—in which virtual forms bleed into the real of war and shared interfaces link the realms of killing and gaming—the question seems ever more pressing. In some important sense, as I have hoped to suggest, the "real" of war has never been apprehended apart from its modes of mediation. Nonetheless, while for some people the waging of war may begin to look and even feel more like a game, for others, the material realities of violence on the ground endure, in ways that remain incalculable.

ACKNOWLEDGMENTS

My greatest debt is to the many scholars in multiple fields whose attentive and insightful analyses have provided the foundation for my own thinking on questions of war and representation across the years. There has been much probing and important work undertaken in the area of war and media studies and I have learned from and been inspired by these efforts. In addition, my thanks go to Leslie Mitchner for her early support of this project, to Nicole Solano for ably taking up the reins, and to all the excellent folks at Rutgers University Press. I'm particularly grateful to Quick Takes series editors Wheeler Winston Dixon and Gwendolyn Audrey Foster for their interest, enthusiasm, and timely, helpful feedback; and to the anonymous reviewer for incisive and extremely generous engagement with the project, and very useful suggestions for its improvement. Lastly, warmest and deepest thanks to all my family, for gamely tolerating my absences and preoccupations, and providing an endless and essential stream of sustenance and support.

FURTHER READING

Arlen, Michael J. *Living-Room War*. New York: Viking, 1969. Print.

Baudrillard, Jean. *The Gulf War Did Not Take Place*. Bloomington: Indiana UP, 1995. Print.

Brown, Charles H. *The Correspondents' War: Journalists in the Spanish American War*. New York: Charles Scribner's Sons, 1967. Print.

Burgoyne, Robert. "Embodiment in the War Film: *Paradise Now* and *The Hurt Locker*." *Journal of War & Culture Studies* 5.1 (2012): 7–19. Print.

———. "The Violated Body: Affective Experience and Somatic Intensity in *Zero Dark Thirty*." *The Philosophy of War Films*. Ed. David LaRocca. Lexington: UP of Kentucky, 2014. 247–60. Print.

Corliss, Richard. "Viet Nam, the Way It Really Was, on Film." *Time* 26 Jan. 1987: 56–61. Print.

DeBauche, Leslie. *Reel Patriotism: The Movies and World War I*. Madison: U of Wisconsin P, 1997. Print.

Dittmar, Linda, and Gene Michaud, eds. *From Hanoi to Hollywood: The Vietnam War in American Film*. New Brunswick, NJ: Rutgers UP, 1990. Print.

Donovan, Tristan. *Replay: The History of Video Games*. Lewes, UK: Yellow Ant, 2010.

Elder, Betty Doak. "War Games: Recruits and their Critics Draw Battle Lines over Authenticity." *History News* 36.8 (1981): 8–12. Print.

Evangelista, Matthew. "Manipulation and Memory in John Huston's *The Battle of San Pietro*." *Film & History* 46.1 (2016): 4–20. Print.

Galison, Peter. "The Ontology of the Enemy: Norbert Wiener and the Cybernetic Vision." *Critical Inquiry* 21.1 (1994): 228–66. Print.

Galloway, Alexander R. *Gaming: Essays on Algorithmic Culture*. Minneapolis: U of Minnesota P, 2006. Print.

Hall, Dennis. "Civil War Reenactors and the Postmodern Sense of History." *Journal of American Culture* 17.3 (1994): 7–11. Print.

Harrigan, Pat, and Matthew G. Kirschenbaum, eds. *Zones of Control: Perspectives on Wargaming*. Cambridge, MA: MIT P, 2016. Print.

Higashi, Sumiko. "Melodrama, Realism, and Race: World War II Newsreels and Propaganda Film." *Cinema Journal* 37.3 (1998): 38–61. Print.

Huhtamo, Erkki, and Roger F. Malina. *Illusions in Motion: A Media Archaeology of the Moving Panorama and Related Spectacles*. Cambridge, MA: MIT P, 2013. Print.

Huntemann, Nina B., and Matthew Thomas Payne, eds. *Joystick Soldiers: The Politics of Play in Military Video Games*. New York: Routledge, 2010. Print.

Jeffords, Susan, and Lauren Rabinovitz, eds. *Seeing through the Media: The Persian Gulf War*. New Brunswick, NJ: Rutgers UP, 1994. Print.

King, Geoff. "Seriously Spectacular: 'Authenticity' and 'Art' in the War Epic." *Spectacular Narratives: Hollywood in the Age of the Blockbuster*. London: I. B. Tauris, 2000. 117–42. Print.

Kline, Stephen, Nick Dyer-Witheford, and Greig de Peuter. *Digital Play: The Interaction of Technology, Culture, and Marketing*. Montreal: McGill-Queen's UP, 2003. Print.

Lowood, Henry. "Impotence and Agency: Computer Games as a Post-9/11 Battlefield." *Computer Games as a Sociocultural Phenomenon*. Ed. Andreas Jahn-Sudmann and Ralf Stockmann. New York: Palgrave Macmillan, 2008. 78–86. Print.

Marcus, Daniel. "William Wyler's World War II Films and the Bombing of Civilian Populations." *Historical Journal of Film, Radio and Television* 29.1 (2009): 79–90. Print.

Morgan, Thomas D. "Wargames: Training for War." *Army History* 19 (1991): 32–35. Print.

Orgeron, Marsha. "Filming the Marines in the Pacific: An Interview with World War II Cinematographer Norman Hatch." *Historical Journal of Film, Radio and Television* 28.2 (2008): 153–73. Print.

Oriard, Michael. *Reading Football: How the Popular Press Created an American Spectacle*. Chapel Hill: U of North Carolina P, 1998. Print.

Perla, Peter. *The Art of Wargaming*. Annapolis, MD: Naval Institute P, 1990. Print.

Reddin, Paul. *Wild West Shows*. Urbana: U of Illinois P, 1999.

Sabin, Philip. *Simulating War: Studying Conflict through Simulation Games*. London: Continuum, 2012. Print.

Slocum, J. David, ed. *Hollywood and War: The Film Reader.* New York: Routledge, 2006. Print.

Stam, Robert. "Mobilizing Fictions: The Gulf War, the Media and the Recruitment of the Spectator." *Public Culture* 4.2 (1992): 101–26. Print.

Vargas, Jose Antonio. "Virtual Reality Prepares Soldiers for Real War." *Washington Post* 14 Feb. 2006. Web.

Voorhees, Gerald A., Josh Call, and Katie Whitlock, eds. *Guns, Grenades, and Grunts: First-Person Shooter Games.* New York: Continuum, 2012. Print.

Waller, Fred. "The Waller Flexible Gunnery Trainer." 1945. *in70mm* 1 Sept. 2010. Web.

"War Games: The Patriotic Clubs Training Young Americans: In Pictures." *Guardian* 13 Mar. 2018. Web.

WORKS CITED

Abel, Richard. "Charge and Countercharge: 'Documentary' War Pictures in the USA, 1914–1916." *Film History* 22 (2010): 366–88. Print.

Agee, James. *Agee on Film*. Vol. 1. New York: Grosset and Dunlap, 1967. Print.

Allen, Robertson. *America's Digital Army: Games at Work and War*. Lincoln: U of Nebraska P, 2017. Print.

Allen, Thomas B. *War Games*. New York: McGraw-Hill, 1987. Print.

Allison, Tanine. *Destructive Sublime: World War II in American Film and Media*. New Brunswick, NJ: Rutgers UP, 2018. Print.

Andersen, Robin. *A Century of Media, a Century of War*. New York: Peter Lang, 2006. Print.

Andersen, Robin, and Marin Kurti. "From *America's Army* to *Call of Duty*: Doing Battle with the Military Entertainment Complex." *Democratic Communiqué* 23.1 (2009): 45–65. Print.

Apel, Dora. *War Culture and the Contest of Images*. New Brunswick, NJ: Rutgers UP, 2012. Print.

Ascherson, Neal. "Missing in Action." *Observer* 6 Sept. 1998: C7. Print.

Asquith, Anthony. "Realler than the Real Thing." *Cine-Technician* 53 (Mar.–Apr. 1945): 25–27. Print.

Berg, Rick. "Losing Vietnam: Covering the War in an Age of Technology." *From Hanoi to Hollywood*. Ed. Linda Dittmar and Gene Michaud. New Brunswick, NJ: Rutgers UP, 1990. 41–68. Print.

BIS (Bohemia Interactive Simulations). "Virtual Battlespace." Web.

Borges, Jorge Luis. "On Exactitude in Science." 1946. *Collected Fictions*. Trans. Andrew Hurley. New York: Penguin Books, 1998. 325. Print.

Bourke, Joanna. *Wounding the World: How Military Violence and War-Play Invade Our Lives*. London: Virago, 2014. Print.

Bradshaw, Peter. "*They Shall Not Grow Old* Review: Peter Jackson's Electrifying Journey into the First World War Trenches." *Guardian* 16 Oct. 2018. Web.

Brown, John S. Foreword. *The Modern Louisiana Maneuvers*. By James L. Yarrison. U.S. Army. Web.

Brown, Kenneth D. "Modelling for War? Toy Soldiers in Late Victorian and Edwardian Britain." *Journal of Social History* 24.2 (1990): 237–54. Print.

Conley, Brian. "Troubling the Magic Circle: *Miniature War in Iraq*." *Zones of Control*. Ed. Pat Harrigan and Matthew G. Kirschenbaum. Cambridge, MA: MIT P, 2016. 409–18. Print.

Cooper, Helene. "Everyone Loves a Parade." *New York Times* 27 May 2018. Web.

Crandall, Jordan. "On Warfare and Representation." *Economising Culture*. Ed. Geoff Cox, Joasia Krysa, and Anya Lewin. New York: Autonomedia, 2004. 215–22. Print.

Crane, Stephen. *The Red Badge of Courage: An Episode of the American Civil War*. 1895. New York: Signet, 1960. Print.

Crogan, Patrick. *Gameplay Mode: War, Simulation, and Technoculture*. Minneapolis: U of Minnesota P, 2011. Print.

Dao, James. "Drone Pilots Are Found to Get Stress Disorders Much as Those in Combat Do." *New York Times* 22 Feb. 2013. Web.

Decker, Todd. *Hymns for the Fallen: Combat Movie Music and Sound after Vietnam*. Berkeley: U of California P, 2017. Print.

Der Derian, James. *Virtuous War*. Boulder, CO: Westview, 2001. Print.

Doherty, Thomas. *Projections of War: Hollywood, American Culture, and World War II*. New York: Columbia UP, 1993. Print.

Dyer-Witheford, Nick, and Greig de Peuter. *Games of Empire: Global Capitalism and Video Games*. Minneapolis: U of Minnesota P, 2009. Print.

Eagle, Jonna. *Imperial Affects: Sensational Melodrama and the Attractions of American Cinema*. New Brunswick, NJ: Rutgers UP, 2017. Print.

Fillis, Frank E. *The South African Boer War Exhibition: The Greatest and Most Realistic Military Spectacle Known in the History of the World*. St. Louis: Woodward and Tiernan, 1904. Print.

Gapps, Stephen. "Mobile Monuments: A View of Historical Reenactment and Authenticity from Inside the Costume Cupboard of History." *Rethinking History* 13.3 (2009): 395–409. Print.

Ghamari-Tabrizi, Sharon. "The Convergence of the Pentagon and Hollywood: The Next Generation of Military Training Simulations." *Memory Bytes*. Ed. Lauren Rabinovitz and Abraham Geil. Durham, NC: Duke UP, 2003. 150–73. Print.

———. "Simulating the Unthinkable: Gaming Future War in the 1950s and 1960s." *Social Studies of Science* 30.2 (2000): 163–223. Print.

Gibson, James William. *Warrior Dreams: Violence and Manhood in Post-Vietnam America*. New York: Hill and Wang, 1994. Print.

Gold, Herbert. "The Real Thing." *Film: Book 2: Films of Peace and War*. Ed. Robert Hughes. New York: Grove, 1962. 19–21. Print.

Goodgame, Dan. "How the War Was Won." *Time* 26 Jan. 1987: 58. Print.

Grischkowsky, Thomas. "Found! Photographs from MoMA's 1944 *Normal Bel Geddes' War Maneuver Models* Exhibition." *Inside/Out* 25 Feb. 2015. Web.

Haggith, Toby. "D-Day Filming for Real." *Film History* 14 (2002): 332–53. Print.

Hallin, Daniel. *The Uncensored War: The Media and Vietnam*. Berkeley: U of California P, 1989. Print.

Halter, Ed. *From Sun Tzu to Xbox: War and Video Games*. New York: Thunder's Mouth, 2006. Print.

Hammond, Michael. *The Big Show: British Cinema Culture in the Great War 1914–1918*. Exeter, UK: U of Exeter P, 2006. Print.

———. "*Saving Private Ryan's* 'Special Affect.'" *Action and*

Adventure Cinema. Ed. Yvonne Tasker. London: Routledge, 2004. 153–66. Print.
Hernandez, Christopher. "Mortuary Affairs Unit Trains Soldiers on Simulating Combat Wounds." U.S. Army. Web.
Herr, Michael. *Dispatches*. New York: Avon, 1978. Print.
Horwitz, Tony. *Confederates in the Attic: Dispatches from the Unfinished Civil War*. New York: Vintage, 1999. Print.
James, David E. "Documenting the Vietnam War." *From Hanoi to Hollywood*. Ed. Linda Dittmar and Gene Michaud. New Brunswick, NJ: Rutgers UP, 1990. 239–54. Print.
Jolin, Dan. "The Rise and Rise of Tabletop Gaming." *Guardian* 25 Sept. 2016. Web.
Koszarski, Richard. "Subway Commandos: Hollywood Filmmakers at the Signal Corps Photographer Center." *Film History* 14 (2002): 296–315. Print.
Lenoir, Tim, and Luke Caldwell. *The Military-Entertainment Complex*. Cambridge, MA: Harvard UP, 2018. Print.
Lenoir, Tim, and Henry Lowood. "Theaters of War: The Military-Entertainment Complex." Stanford University. Jan. 2003. Web.
Levinthal, David. "War Games." *Zones of Control*. Ed. Pat Harrigan and Matthew G. Kirschenbaum. Cambridge, MA: MIT P, 2016. 399–408. Print.
Lukas, Scott A. "Behind the Barrel: Reading the Video Game Gun." *Joystick Soldiers*. Ed. Nina B. Huntemann and Matthew Thomas Payne. New York: Routledge, 2010. 75–90. Print.
Magnuson, Stew. "Air Warriors (Revamped Flag Exercises

Reflect New Missions)." *National Defense* 1 Dec. 2006. Web.

Manaugh, Geoff, and Nicola Twilley. "It's Artificial Afghanistan: A Simulated Battlefield in the Mojave Desert." *Atlantic* 18 May 2013. Web.

Maslowski, Peter. *Armed with Cameras: The American Military Photographers of World War II*. New York: Free P, 1993. Print.

McSorley, Kevin. "Helmetcams, Militarized Sensation, and 'Somatic War.'" *Journal of War and Culture Studies* 5.1 (2012): 47–58. Print.

Mead, Corey. *War Play: Video Games and the Future of Armed Conflict*. New York: Houghton Mifflin Harcourt, 2013. Print.

Mieszkowski, Jan. "War, with Popcorn." *Chronicle of Higher Education* 18 July 2014. Web.

———. *Watching War*. Stanford, CA: Stanford UP, 2012. Print.

Nakamura, Tetsuya. "The Fundamental Gap between Tabletop Simulation Games and the 'Truth.'" *Zones of Control*. Ed. Pat Harrigan and Matthew G. Kirschenbaum. Cambridge, MA: MIT P, 2016. 43–48. Print.

Nellis Air Force Base. "Exercises and Flight Operations." Web.

———. "Green Flag-West." Web.

"New War Game in America: Shoot the Grass Shacks." *Los Angeles Times* 17 Mar. 1968: F4. Print.

NTC (National Training Center) and Fort Irwin. "NTC Tours." Web.

Parks, Lisa. *Rethinking Media Coverage: Vertical Mediation and the War on Terror*. New York: Routledge, 2018. Print.

Payne, Matthew Thomas. *Playing War: Military Video Games after 9/11*. New York: New York UP, 2016. Print.

Peirce, Charles. *Collected Papers of Charles Sanders Peirce*. Ed. Charles Hartshorne and Paul Weiss. Vol. 4. Cambridge, MA: Harvard UP, 1933. Print.

Perla, Peter P. "Operations Research, Systems Analysis, and Wargaming: Riding the Cycle of Research." *Zones of Control*. Ed. Pat Harrigan and Matthew G. Kirschenbaum. Cambridge, MA: MIT P, 2016. 159–82. Print.

Perry, Mark. "Louisiana Maneuvers (1940–41)." *Military History* 25 Nov. 2008. Web.

Perry, Tony. "Marine Exercise Sends a Message to Milosevic." *Los Angeles Times* 15 Apr. 1999. Web.

Peterson, Jon. "A Game Out of All Proportions: How a Hobby Miniaturized War." *Zones of Control*. Ed. Pat Harrigan and Matthew G. Kirschenbaum. Cambridge, MA: MIT P, 2016. 3–32. Print.

———. *Playing at the World*. San Diego, CA: Unreason, 2012. Print.

Platoni, Kara. "The Pentagon Goes to the Video Arcade." *Progressive* 1 July 1999: 27. Print.

Ramirez, Enrique. "Larger Scales of Norman Bel Geddes." *a456* 24 Aug. 2010. Web.

Ressner, Jeffrey. "War Is Hell." *DGA Quarterly* Fall 2011. Web.

Rosenthal, Daniel J., and Loren DeJonge Schulman. "Trump's Secret War on Terror." *Atlantic* 10 Aug. 2018. Web.

Rubin, Steven Jay. *Combat Films: American Realism, 1945–2010*. Jefferson, NC: McFarland, 2011. Print.

Schiesel, Seth. "On Maneuvers with the Army's Game Squad." *New York Times* 17 Feb. 2005. Web.

Schmidt, Michael S. "Air Force, Running Low on Drone Pilots, Turns to Contractors in Terror Fight." *New York Times* 5 Sept. 2016. Web.

Scott, A. O. "Soldiers on a Live Wire between Peril and Protocol." *New York Times* 25 June 2009. Web.

Shikina, Rob. "Sea-to-Shore Show of Force." *Honolulu Star Advertiser* 30 July 2018: A1+. Print.

Stahl, Roger. *Militainment, Inc.: War, Media, and Popular Culture*. New York: Routledge, 2010. Print.

———. *Through the Crosshairs: War, Visual Culture and the Weaponized Gaze*. New Brunswick, NJ: Rutgers UP, 2018. Print.

Strategic Operations. Home page. Web.

Sturken, Marita. "Reenactment and the Making of History: The Vietnam War as Docudrama." *Tangled Memories: The Vietnam War, the AIDS Epidemic, and the Politics of Remembering*. Berkeley: U of California P, 1997. 85–121. Print.

Suellentrop, Chris. "War Games." *New York Times Magazine* 8 Sept. 2010. Web.

Swofford, Anthony. "'Full Metal Jacket' Seduced My Generation and Sent Us to War." *New York Times Magazine* 18 Apr. 2018. Web.

Taylor, Giles. "A Military Use for Widescreen Cinema: Training the Body through Immersive Media." *Velvet Light Trap* 72 (Fall 2013): 17–32. Print.

Team Orlando. "Strengthening the Warfighter through Simulation." Web.

Thompson, Jenny. *War Games: Inside the World of Twentieth-Century War Reenactors*. Washington, DC: Smithsonian Books, 2004. Print.

Thomson, Matthew. "Underdog to Overmatch: Computer Games and Military Transformation." *Popular Communication* 7 (2009): 92–106. Print.

Train, Brian, and Volko Ruhnke. "Chess, Go, and Vietnam: Gaming Modern Insurgency." *Zones of Control*. Ed. Pat Harrigan and Matthew G. Kirschenbaum. Cambridge, MA: MIT P, 2016. 513–30. Print.

Tran, Edmond. "*God of War*: Immersive HUD Mode Is the Best Way to Play." *Gamespot* 28 Apr. 2018. Web.

Troianovski, Anton, Anna Fifield, and Paul Stone. "War Games and Business Deals: Russia, China Send a Signal to Washington." *Washington Post* 11 Sept. 2018. Web.

Turner, Rory. "Bloodless Battles: The Civil War Reenacted." *Drama Review* 34.4 (1990): 123–36. Print.

———. "The Play of History: Civil War Reenactments and Their Use of the Past." *Folklore Forum* 22.1–2 (1989): 54–61. Print.

"U.S. Weapons Put on Show by Museum." *Chicago Tribune* 15 Mar. 1968: D6. Print.

Van Creveld, Martin. *Wargames: From Gladiators to Gigabytes*. Cambridge: Cambridge UP, 2013. Print.

Virilio, Paul. *War and Cinema: The Logistics of Perception*. London: Verso, 1989. Print.

Voorhees, Gerald. "Monsters, Nazis, and Tangos: The Normalization of the First-Person Shooter." *Guns, Grenades,*

and Grunts. Ed. Gerald A. Voorhees, Josh Call, and Katie Whitlock. New York: Continuum, 2012. 89–112. Print.
Wells, H. G. *Little Wars: A Game for Boys from Twelve Years of Age to One Hundred and Fifty and for That More Intelligent Sort of Girl Who Likes Boys' Games and Books*. 1913. Project Gutenberg. Web.
White, Geoffrey M., and Jane Yi. "*December 7th*: Race and Nation in Wartime Documentary." *Classic Hollywood, Classic Whiteness*. Ed. Daniel Bernardi. Minneapolis: U of Minnesota P, 2001. 301–38. Print.
Wingfield, Nick. "High-Tech Push Has Board Games Rolling Again." *New York Times* 5 May 2014. Web.
Youra, Steven. "James Agee on Films and the Theater of War." *Film Criticism* 10.1 (1985): 18–31. Print.
Zimmerman, Patricia. "Cameras and Guns, 1941–1949." *Reel Families: A Social History of Amateur Film*. Bloomington: Indiana UP, 1995. 90–111. Print.

INDEX

ABOUT THE AUTHOR

Jonna Eagle is an associate professor of film and media in the Department of American Studies at the University of Hawai'i at Mānoa, where she teaches courses on war and media, American cinema, critical and cultural theory, and social and cultural history. Her previous publications include *Imperial Affects: Sensational Melodrama and the Attractions of American Cinema* (2017), also from Rutgers University Press. She lives with her family in Honolulu.

